Saint Augustine on the Resurrection of Christ

Saint Augustine on the Resurrection of Christ

Teaching, Rhetoric, and Reception

GERALD O'COLLINS, SJ

UNIVERSITY PRESS

Great Clarendon Street, Oxford, OX2 6DP,
United Kingdom

Oxford University Press is a department of the University of Oxford.
It furthers the University's objective of excellence in research, scholarship,
and education by publishing worldwide. Oxford is a registered trade mark of
Oxford University Press in the UK and in certain other countries

© Gerald O'Collins, SJ 2017

The moral rights of the author have been asserted

First Edition published in 2017

All rights reserved. No part of this publication may be reproduced, stored in
a retrieval system, or transmitted, in any form or by any means, without the
prior permission in writing of Oxford University Press, or as expressly permitted
by law, by licence or under terms agreed with the appropriate reprographics
rights organization. Enquiries concerning reproduction outside the scope of the
above should be sent to the Rights Department, Oxford University Press, at the
address above

You must not circulate this work in any other form
and you must impose this same condition on any acquirer

Published in the United States of America by Oxford University Press
198 Madison Avenue, New York, NY 10016, United States of America

British Library Cataloguing in Publication Data

Data available

Library of Congress Control Number: 2016956620

ISBN 978-0-19-879954-2

Preface

The remarkable life of St Augustine of Hippo (354–430) spanned a period dense with debates about the personal identity and natures of Jesus Christ. The Christian Church passed one theological milestone after another as controversies led to (and followed) what the First Council of Nicaea (325), the First Council of Constantinople (381), the Council of Ephesus (431), and the Council of Chalcedon (451) taught about Christ. He is truly divine (Nicaea I); he is fully human (Constantinople I); his divinity and humanity, while not separated (Ephesus), are not confused (Chalcedon).

Before the time of Augustine's teaching and writing ministry and shortly after his death, bishops and others wrote notable tracts on Christ, such as the *De Incarnatione Verbi* by St Athanasius of Alexandria (d. 373), the *Quod unus sit Christus* of Cyril of Alexandria (d. 444), and the *Tomus ad Flavianum* of St Leo the Great (d. 461). But Augustine never produced a particular tract which addressed the Christological issues that emerged in the fourth and fifth centuries. The most extensive passage on Christology comes in *The Trinity* (4.1–5).

To be sure, reflections on Jesus Christ turn up constantly in Augustine's more than 400 extant sermons (biblically rich, often rhetorically dazzling, and long neglected or even unknown), the 252 letters by him (plus forty-nine others addressed to him) that have survived, the *City of God*, *The Trinity*, his works against the Arian heresy, and other writings—not least his longest work, *Expositions of the Psalms*. He was the first to produce a complete commentary on the Psalms, which he expounded as the *vox ad Christum* (the word addressed to Christ), the *vox de Christo* (the word spoken about Christ), and the *vox Christi* (the word spoken by Christ).

Belief in Christ as the incarnate Son of God, who came to mediate between human beings and God through his life, death, resurrection, and ascension was an utterly fundamental condition for Augustine's faith and life. He showed a totally Christ-centred cast of mind. Christ gave meaning to his whole existence, through his being mysteriously united with Christ and the members of the one Body of Christ.

Preaching the message of Christ constituted the central core of Augustine's ministry exercised for those who already belonged to the Church and for others. Yet Augustine never fused into a complete theological work what he held to be the most significant features of his faith in Christ.

This absence of a theological treatise on Christ, along with further reasons, encouraged scholars to come at Augustine's theology from other angles. They devoted themselves rather to studying what he said about free will, grace, the interpretation of Scripture, original sin, predestination, the sacraments, the Trinity, and so forth. To be sure, some scholars have examined the teaching of Augustine on the incarnation, the passion of Christ, his ascension, the resurrection of the body in general, Christ's union with others in the 'Totus Christus (the whole Christ)', and Christological questions that come up in the context of studying the Holy Trinity.

But we still lack studies precisely on Christ's own resurrection from the dead. Very little attention has been directed to what Augustine preached and wrote about the rising of Christ himself and the questions it raises. Christ's resurrection hardly enters, for instance, what Goulven Madec wrote on 'Christus', in Cornelius Mayer (ed.), *Augustinus-Lexikon* (Basel: Schwabe, 1986–94), col. 845–908. The resurrection of Christ is ignored by Basil Studer, *The Grace of God and the Grace of Christ in Augustine of Hippo: Christocentrism or Theocentrism?*, trans. Matthew J. O'Connell (Collegeville, Minn.: Liturgical Press, 1997). In Allan D. Fitzgerald (ed.), *Augustine Through the Ages: An Encyclopedia* (Grand Rapids, Mich.: Eerdmans, 1999), William Mallard has nothing to say about the resurrection in his entry, 'Jesus Christ' (pp. 463–70), while Brian E. Daley's entry 'Resurrection' barely touches Christ's resurrection and attends rather to the resurrection of the body in general (pp. 722–3). In Robert Dodaro and George Lawless (eds.), *Augustine and His Critics: Essays in Honour of Gerald Bonner* (London: Routledge, 2000), Hubertus R. Drobner writes on 'Studying Augustine: An Overview of Recent Research' (pp. 18–34), but has little to report on Christology and nothing at all on the resurrection of Jesus (pp. 27–9).

This study aims to fill this important gap. We will present in Chapter 1 what can be found, here and there in the works of Augustine, about the central importance of faith in Jesus' resurrection from the dead, the agency of Christ's own resurrection, the nature of his risen existence, the impact of his resurrection on others, and his mediatory role as the risen High Priest who is the invisible minister of the sacraments and eternally intercedes for sinful human beings.

Before being converted in 386 and then baptized at Easter 387, Augustine had proved himself to be outstanding as a practitioner of rhetoric, some would say the last great Roman rhetorician. As a Christian priest (391) and bishop (395), he gave himself unsparingly to the public role of preaching and teaching the message of the Gospel. His professional skills as a rhetorician came into play, not least when he justified believing in Christ risen from the dead. He appealed to evidence from created nature, human history, and the experiences and desires of his audience. He exercised his rhetoric not for its own sake, still less to achieve power over his hearers and readers, but to persuade them of the truth and life-giving nature of Easter faith. The second chapter of this book examines the case Augustine, secular rhetorician turned Christian apologist, made for the veracity of the resurrection of Jesus from the dead.

When it seems useful, Chapters 1 and 2 will evaluate Augustine's teaching on and apologetic for the resurrection in the light of later theology. For instance, his argument that for certain, observable historical effects, the only adequate cause is the resurrection of Jesus has continued under somewhat different forms.

The remarkable, three-volume *Oxford Guide to the Historical Reception of Augustine* (Oxford University Press, 2013), edited by Karla Pollmann, has encouraged me to go further in recognizing how to retrieve and receive Augustine's thought. So too has Rowan Williams, who brings Augustine into conversation with such modern thinkers as Hannah Arendt, Reinhold Niebuhr, Martha Nussbaum, and Ludwig Wittgenstein (*On Augustine* (London: Bloomsbury, 2016)). Hence Chapters 3 and 4 will set themselves (a) to illustrate the enduring significance of his teaching and apologetic and (b), where necessary, to update, correct, and supplement Augustine's view of Christ's resurrection.

Thus this book assesses Augustine's thought on Christ's resurrection and then brings him into conversation with later, modern discussion. The aim is to maintain a proper balance between (a) the exposition and (b) a critical reception of Augustine. The book is driven by this dual purpose often exemplified in the *Oxford Guide to the Historical*

Reception of Augustine. Over and over again that work shows how later authors, in areas other than Christ's resurrection, retrieved, adapted, and applied Augustine's teaching and rhetoric. My hope is to produce a cohesive monograph that does something similar for what he said and wrote on Jesus' rising from the dead.

Many years ago, after I delivered my first major lecture on Augustine, several leaders in Augustine studies suggested that I should have specified the dates of various homilies, letters, and other works and indicated at times the nature or length of the work cited. Hence this book includes such specifications. They illuminate, for instance, an even firmer stress by Augustine on the 'fleshly' reality of the resurrection of Christ (and others).

The recent publication by New City Press of good annotated translations of Augustine's works has made my study much easier. For a rich and up-to-date bibliography of works by Augustine and works on Augustine, readers can consult the abundant information provided by Joseph T. Kelley, *What Are They Saying About Augustine?* (Mahwah, NJ: Paulist Press, 2014). For translation from the Bible, this book normally follows the New Revised Standard Version. At the end it includes a select bibliography of publications that concern the resurrection of Jesus Christ in the thought of Augustine and some modern authors. My warm thanks go to four anonymous readers (two for Oxford University Press and two for the Jesuit order). I dedicate my work to the memory of Henry Chadwick, teacher, mentor, and friend par excellence.

Jesuit Theological College, Parkville, Australia
31 July 2016

Contents

List of Abbreviations   xi

1. The Resurrection of the Crucified Jesus: Augustine's Faith   1
2. Arguments for Jesus' Resurrection: Augustine's Rhetoric   32
3. Augustine's Resurrection Faith Updated   60
4. Augustine's Case for the Resurrection Updated   96
5. Final Perspectives   115

Select Bibliography   119
A Biblical Index   123
An Index of Names   126

List of Abbreviations

ABD	D. N. Freedman (ed.), *Anchor Bible Dictionary*, 6 vols. (New York: Doubleday, 1992).
c. Faust.	*Contra Faustum Manichaeum (Answer to Faustus a Manichean)*
civ.	*De Civitate Dei (The City of God)*
doctr. Chr.	*De Doctrina Christiana (Teaching Christianity)*
en. Ps.	*Enarrationes in Psalmos (Expositions of the Psalms)*
ep.	*Epistolae (Letters)*
Io. ev. tr.	*Tractatus in Iohannis Evangelium (Homilies on the Gospel of John)*
NRSV	New Revised Standard Version
Par. parr.	Parallel passage(s) in the Synoptic Gospels
PL	*Patrologia Latina*, ed. J. P. Migne, 221 volumes
REB	Revised English Bible
s.	*Sermones (Sermons)*
Trin.	*De Trinitate (The Trinity)*

1
The Resurrection of the Crucified Jesus
Augustine's Faith

Augustine never wrote a treatise on the resurrection of Jesus Christ. Hence this chapter has no principal source but must draw on various works: *Answer to Faustus a Manichean*, *The City of God*, *Expositions of the Psalms*, *Homilies on the Gospel of John*, *Letters*, *Sermons*, and *The Trinity*. Establishing what is significant in all this material, we will show how Augustine attended to seven major themes when presenting the resurrection of Christ.

(1) Belief in the resurrection of Jesus Christ from the dead is the heart of Christian faith and sets Christians apart from Jews and others. (2) Like the Gospel of John, Augustine highlights Christ's active role in his own resurrection. (3) While Christ's risen existence was 'spiritual' and immortal, his flesh could be handled, and he could eat and drink, even though he did not need to do so. (4) Augustine seems reluctant to state clearly that, while joined to his resurrected 'members', Christ the head will sing with them the praises of God. (5) The risen Christ is both the pledge of coming resurrection for others, and the 'sacrament' effecting their being raised from sin and physical death. (6) The risen Christ is the mediator of new life, and (7) the true minister of the sacraments and the priest who eternally 'intercedes on our behalf'. In expounding these last three points, we will see how, when presenting Christ's resurrection, Augustine to some extent prioritizes *Christus pro nobis* over *Christus in se*.

The Resurrection as the Heart of Christian Faith

Over many years, Augustine highlighted belief in the resurrection of Jesus as the heart of Christian faith, a belief that sets Christians apart from Jews and others. In his *Expositions of the Psalms* (delivered between *c*.392 and *c*.420 AD), for example, he defined the faith of Christians in terms of the resurrection. Commenting on Psalm 101, he insisted:

> The faith of Christians is not triumphant because they believe that Christ died but because they believe that Christ rose again. Even a pagan believes that he died…In what do you really take pride? You believe that Christ is risen and you hope that through Christ you will rise. This is why your faith is triumphant. (en. Ps. 101.7)

Having said that, Augustine at once quoted Paul: 'If you confess with your lips that Jesus is Lord and believe in your heart that God raised him from the dead, you will be saved' (Rom. 10: 9).[1]

When commenting on Psalm 120, Augustine says something very similar. Christ's resurrection defines Christian faith and identity.

> By the passion the Lord passed over from death to life; and opened a way for us who believe in his resurrection, that we too may pass over from death to life. It is no great thing to believe that Christ died: pagans and Jews, and all bad people (*iniqui*) believe that. All of them are sure that he died. The faith of Christians is in the resurrection of Christ. This is what matters to us (*hoc pro magno habemus*), that we believe that he rose from the dead.

Once more Augustine proceeds to quote Romans 10: 9 (en. Ps. 120.6).[2]

In *De Trinitate*, a masterpiece composed from *c*.400 to shortly after 420 AD, Augustine wrote in a similar vein: 'it is faith in its [the flesh of Christ's] resurrection that saves and justifies…it is the resurrection of the Lord's body that gives value to our faith…Even his enemies believe that that body died on the cross of pain, but they do not

---

[1] *Expositions of the Psalms* (99–120), trans. Maria Boulding (Hyde Park, NY: New City Press, 2003), 67; see Trin. 2.29; *The Trinity*, trans. Edmund Hill (Brooklyn, NY: New City Press, 1991), 118.

[2] *Expositions of the Psalms* (99–120), 514–15.

believe that it rose again. We, however, believe it absolutely' (Trin. 2.29).[3]

One could quote further passages from Augustine to illustrate his conviction that belief in Jesus Christ's resurrection fashions and forms the distinctive faith of Christians. Often he appeals to Romans 10: 9 as a scriptural confirmation for this claim. In a sermon preached during the Easter octave of 418 AD, he exhorts the congregation: 'Let us believe in Christ crucified; but in him as the one who rose again on the third day. That's the faith which…distinguishes us from the pagans, distinguishes us from the Jews; the faith by which we believe that Christ has risen from the dead.' At once Augustine cites again the words of Romans 10: 9 (s. 234.3).[4] In a work written (between 408 and 410 AD) against Faustus, a Manichean, he observes: 'Even the pagans, to be sure, believe that Christ died, but the faith proper to Christians is that he rose.' Yet again Augustine goes straight on to quote Romans 10: 9 in support of what he had said (c. Faust. 16.29).[5]

Given this significance assigned to Christ's own resurrection from the dead in establishing the faith and identity of Christians, it is surprising that we lack substantial studies of Augustine's thought in this area.[6] If Augustine matters elsewhere, he also matters in what he

---

[3] *The Trinity*, 118. On the resurrection in *De Trinitate*, see Cristina Simonetti, *La risurrezione nel De Trinitate di Agostino: presenza, formulazione, funzione*, Studia Ephemeridis Augustinianum 73 (Rome: Augustinianum, 2001).

[4] *Sermons* (230–272B), trans. Edmund Hill (New Rochelle, NY: New City Press, 1993), 37. The day before in s. 233.1, Augustine had said something very similar, although this time without referring to Rom. 10: 9: 'The resurrection of Christ is what our faith is firmly based on (*constabilita est*). Both pagans and godless people (*iniqui*) and Jews have believed about the passion of Christ; about his resurrection only Christians' (ibid. 32). In a sermon preached after 412 AD, Augustine insisted: 'the resurrection of the Lord Jesus Christ is the distinctive mark (*forma*) of the Christian faith…both friends and enemies have believed that Christ was crucified and died; that he rose again, only his friends have known'. Hence he concluded: 'this is what defines our faith, the resurrection of our Lord Jesus Christ' (s. 229H.1, 3; *Sermons* (184–229Z), trans. Edmund Hill (New Rochelle, NY: New City Press, 1993), 295, 297.

[5] *Answer to Faustus a Manichean*, trans. Roland J. Teske (Hyde Park, NY: New City Press, 2007), 222.

[6] Some scholars have taken up related areas—in particular, Mamerto Alfeche in several articles: e.g. 'The Rising of the Dead in the Work of Augustine (1 Cor.

said and wrote about Christ's own rising from the dead. What has already been cited from Augustine brings up at least two themes: Christ's active role in his resurrection, and his opening the way by which 'we too may pass over from death to life'. Let us address the former question, leaving the latter for reflection under (6) below.

Christ's Active Role in his Resurrection

Years ago Rudolf Bultmann pointed out how the adjectival clause 'who raised him [Jesus] from the dead' turns up as 'a formula-like attribute of God' in the certainly authentic letters of Paul and elsewhere in the New Testament (e.g. 1 Pet. 1: 21).[7] The apostle begins his Letter to the Galatians with an appeal to 'God the Father who raised him [Jesus] from the dead' (1: 1). He warns the Corinthians against fornication by recalling their bodily destiny: 'God raised the Lord and will also raise us up with his power' (1 Cor. 6: 14). In Pauline terms, God may be said simply to have raised Jesus from the dead (Rom. 10: 9), or to have raised him by his 'glory' (Rom. 6: 4), through his 'Spirit' (Rom. 8: 11), or by his 'power' (1 Cor. 6: 14).[8] Paul speaks of Christ's

---

15: 35–57)', *Augustiniana* 39 (1989), 54–98; M. Alfeche, 'Augustine's Discussions with Philosophers on the Resurrection of the Body', *Augustiniana* 45 (1995), 95–140; see also Marie-François Berrouard, *L'Integrité de la nature humaine du Christ après sa resurrection* (Paris: Institut d'Études Augustiniennes, 1977); William H. Marrevee, *The Ascension of Christ in the Works of St Augustine* (Ottawa: University of Ottawa Press, 1967). But I know only one (brief) scholarly study on the topic of the resurrection of Christ himself in the thought of Augustine, a chapter in a book that limits itself to Augustine's sermons: Andrea Bizzozero, *Il mistero pasquale di Gesù Cristo e l'esistenza credente nei Sermones di Agostino* (Frankfurt: Peter Lang, 2010), 191–216; I thank Simon Wayte for this reference.

[7] R. Bultmann, *Theology of the New Testament*, trans. Kendrick Grobel, i (London: SCM Press, 1952), 81. See also Lidija Novakovic, 'The God Who Raised Jesus from the Dead: Toward a Theology of Resurrection', in Jason A. Whitlark et al. (eds.), *Interpretation and the Claim of the Text: Resourcing New Testament Theology* (Waco, TX: Baylor University Press, 2014), 17–28.

[8] All these examples use active forms of *egeirō*, except for Rom. 6: 4, where the verb is in the aorist passive, *ēgerthē* ('he was raised'). Elsewhere some aorist passive forms of this verb can or, at times, should be translated intransitively as 'he rose';

risen existence as life 'out of the power of God' (2 Cor. 13: 4). This merges with the notion of Christ's risen state being 'life for God' (Rom. 6: 10).

Later New Testament authors attribute to Christ an increasingly active role in his resurrection. In the Markan predictions of death and resurrection, the Son of Man 'will rise', presumably by his own power (Mk. 8: 31; 9: 31; 10: 34). This developing role for Jesus reaches a highpoint in the Fourth Gospel. He is the agent who will raise others (Jn. 5: 21, 28–9; 6: 39–40). Second, he names himself as the agent of his own resurrection (Jn. 2: 19; 10: 17–18). Finally, the resurrection is simply identified with him: 'I am the resurrection' (Jn. 11: 25).

Augustine characteristically followed later New Testament usage. In an Easter sermon of 391 AD, he presented Jesus rising through his own divine power and quoted in support John 10: 17–18 (s. 375B.2).[9] Twenty years later, in a long sermon on the resurrection of the dead he cited John 10: 18 and proclaimed Jesus as having risen 'by his divine power' (s. 362.12).[10] Augustine, as we saw above, often quoted Romans 10: 9 ('God raised him [Jesus] from the dead'), and in the same sermon of 411 (s. 362.24) also cited Romans 8: 10–11: 'if the Spirit of him who *raised Jesus from the dead* dwells in you, he who *raised Jesus from the dead* will give life to our mortal bodies through his Spirit who dwells in you' (emphasis added).[11] Yet, instead of following Paul and representing Jesus' resurrection as an act of God (the Father) through the Holy Spirit, Augustine left the apostle behind and

---

see Daniel Kendall and Gerald O'Collins, 'Christ's Resurrection and the Aorist Passive of *egeirō*', *Gregorianum* 74 (1993), 725–35.

[9] *Sermons* (341–400), trans. Edmund Hill (New Rochelle, NY: New City Press, 1995), 333. Echoing but not citing Jn. 10. 17–18, Augustine wrote to a certain Januarius around 400 AD: 'he [Christ] had the power to lay down his life and to take it up again' (ep. 55.16; *Letters 1–99*, trans. Roland J. Teske (Hyde Park, NY: New City Press, 2001), 224). Augustine's letters, no less than his sermons, constituted a public forum for expounding Christian teaching; see Jennifer Ebbeler, *Disciplining Christians: Correction and Community in Augustine's Letters* (Oxford: Oxford University Press, 2012).

[10] *Sermons* (341–400), 249. As Augustine puts it in *De Trinitate*, he 'revived his own dead flesh' (Trin. 4.17; *Trinity*, 164).

[11] *Sermons* (341–400), 260.

expressly took up the language of John about Christ's own divine power effecting his resurrection. A sermon from 418 provides another, even more startling example where Augustine quotes from Paul that 'God raised him [Jesus] from the dead' (Rom. 10: 9), but introduces the apostle's words by depicting the resurrection as the action of Jesus himself ('we believe that Christ has risen from the dead') and by glossing the passage as if Paul had spoken of such an action: 'Hold firmly in your hearts, profess it with your lips, that Christ has risen from the dead' (s. 234.3).[12]

At times Augustine expressed the self-resurrection of Christ vividly and vigorously: 'he endured death as a lamb, he devoured it as a lion' (s. 375A.1).[13] A sermon of 418 AD used the same image but turned Christ into a lion-hunter: 'he slew death…Like the greatest of hunters, he caught hold of the lion, and killed it' (s. 233.4).[14] In a sermon on the ascension probably preached in 425 AD, Augustine cited Psalm 19: 5 ('he exulted like a giant') and said of Christ: 'he smashed the gates of hell; he came out and ascended' (s. 377.1).[15]

The New Life of Christ: Before the Ascension

At the end of a sermon preached during the Easter octave of either 412 or 413, Augustine put into the mouth of the risen Christ the following invitation:

> I'm inviting you to my life, where nobody dies, where life is truly happy, where food doesn't go bad…that's where I am inviting you, to the region of the angels, to the friendship of the Father and the Holy Spirit, to the everlasting supper, to be my brothers and sisters, to be, in a word, myself. I'm inviting you to my life. (s. 231.5)[16]

---

[12] *Sermons* (230–272B), 37.
[13] *Sermons* (341–400), 330; this sermon on the sacraments was probably preached in 397 AD.
[14] *Sermons* (230–272B), 34.   [15] *Sermons* (341–400), 351.
[16] *Sermons* (230–272B), 22.

The Resurrection of the Crucified Jesus 7

But what is 'my life' like? What did Augustine say about the risen existence and activities of Christ himself—first, after the resurrection and before the ascension?

In a long sermon on the creed probably preached in 425 AD, Augustine refers to the story of Lazarus being brought back to life (Jn. 11: 38–44) and says laconically: 'Lazarus also rose again, and is dead; Christ rose again, and dies no more' (s. 398.9).[17] Or, as Augustine puts matters in responding to Faustus, a Manichean, 'Christ's flesh rose on the third day and will never die again' (c. Faust. 29.2).[18] In a sermon preached in 411 AD and so during the time when he composed *Answer to Faustus*, Augustine speaks of the risen Christ 'revealing to them [the disciples] the true reality of his flesh: its weakness shown on the cross, its immortality in rising from the tomb' (s. 262.1).[19] The Son of God, he writes in *De Trinitate*, now has 'an immortal body' (Trin. 4.24).[20] A letter written in 419 or 420 AD to Consentius, a Catholic layman in the Balearic Islands, speaks of Christ's risen body being 'spiritual' and 'incorruptible' (ep. 205.8–10).[21]

If the risen Christ is now immortal and so no longer liable to decay and death,[22] what can be said positively about his situation? In an

---

[17] *Sermons* (341–400), 450.

[18] *Answer to Faustus*, 399. In *The City of God* (written between 412/13 and 426/27 AD), Augustine refers to 1 Cor. 15: 45 ('the last Adam became a life-giving spirit'), and says that Christ rose 'from the dead with the result that he would no longer die again' (civ. 13.23; *The City of God XI–XXII*, trans. William Babcock (Hyde Park, NY: New City Press, 2013), 91).

[19] *Sermons* (230–272B), 216.

[20] *Trinity*, 390. See Richard A. Norris, 'Immortality', in Allan D. Fitzgerald (ed.), *Augustine Through the Ages: An Encyclopedia* (Grand Rapids, MI: Eerdmans, 1999), 444–5.

[21] *Letters 156–210*, trans. Roland J. Teske (Hyde Park, NY: New City Press, 2004), 381; see Frederick Van Fleteren, 'Spiritual Being', in Fitzgerald (ed.), *Augustine Through the Ages*, 812–13.

[22] For Augustine, the body of Christ in the tomb was already exempt from decay. In a letter written to a priest Deogratias (between 406 and 412), Augustine said: 'the body of Christ rose on the third day without having decomposed by decay or corruption'. He contrasted this with 'our bodies', which 'will be restored after a long time from some confused state into which they were broken down and disappeared' (ep. 102.5; *Letters 100–155*, trans. Roland J. Teske (Hyde Park, NY: New City Press, 2003), 23).

earlier, long sermon on the resurrection of the dead (from 411 AD) cited above, Augustine states positively: 'Our Lord rose again in the very same body in which he had been buried' (s. 362.10)—a statement that Augustine goes on to repeat in this sermon (s. 362.14).[23] In *The City of God*, Augustine takes matters further by qualifying as 'certainly true' the claim that Christ 'rose' not only in the very same body but also 'with the *very same bodily size* that he had when he died' (civ. 22.15; emphasis added).[24] One detects here something similar to the move Augustine also made in *The City of God* towards specifying resurrected existence in terms of male and female bodies; we will see this later.

It is only occasionally that Augustine notes that 'the very same body' was also a different kind of body, one that was no longer constrained by the normal limits of human bodies. He recalls how 'the doors were closed' when Jesus appeared to the disciples (Jn. 20: 19). Like many later commentators, he explains (in a sermon preached in 411 AD): Jesus 'entered alive *through* closed doors' (s. 376.1; emphasis added).[25] Such a comment inevitably raises questions about the possibility or impossibility of two bodies occupying the same space at the same time. Augustine's comment slips over the fact that the evangelist

---

[23] *Sermons* (230–272B), 247, 250. In a sermon preached six years later (in 417 AD), Augustine assured his congregation that 'what was restored to their [the disciples'] sight after the resurrection was the very same thing that had been taken from them by the cross' (s. 264.2; *Sermons* (230–272B), 226). In a letter written a few years earlier (between 406 and 412), Augustine wrote of the disciples seeing 'the very same body' that 'they had seen crucified' (ep. 102.7; *Letters 100–155*, 24). More than two centuries earlier St Irenaeus had, apropos of resurrection in general, likewise spoken of 'the same body': 'With what body will the dead rise? Certainly with the same body in which they died; otherwise those who rise would not be the same persons who previously died' (*Adversus haereses*, 5.13.1).

[24] *City of God XI–XXII*, 525. See A. D. Fitzgerald, 'Body', in *Augustine Through the Ages*, 105–7; and David G. Hunter, 'Augustine on the Body', in Mark Vessey (ed.), *A Companion to Augustine* (Oxford: Wiley-Blackwell, 2012), 352–64.

[25] *Sermons* (341–400), 346; Augustine says the same in s. 191.2 (*Sermons* (184–229Z), 43), and civ. 22.8 (*City of God XI–XXII*, 515). For a modern example of this explanation, see C. K. Barrett, *The Gospel According to John*, 2nd edn. (London: SPCK, 1978), 568: 'mentioning that the doors were shut was to suggest the mysterious power of the risen Jesus, who was at once sufficiently corporeal to show his wounds and sufficiently immaterial to enter through closed doors'.

does *not* say that Jesus passed through closed doors, but simply indicates that such a material barrier cannot prevent the risen Lord from showing himself to his disciples. He appears (Jn. 20: 19) and disappears (Lk. 24: 31) at will.

In *The City of God* Augustine discusses risen bodies being 'spiritual', not 'because they will cease to be bodies, but because they will be sustained by a life-giving spirit'. They will retain 'the substance of flesh' but now 'suited for dwelling in heaven'. This 'will come about due not to a loss in its [the body's] nature but to a change in its quality' (civ. 13.22, 23).[26] He presses on to say that the 'spiritual' body is 'the kind of body that has already preceded us in Christ, as our head' (civ. 13.23).[27] Later in *The City of God*, Augustine writes: 'Brightness was not lacking in Christ's body when he rose but was simply hidden from the eyes of the disciples. For the weakness of human sight could not bear such brightness at the point when it was right for Christ to be seen by the disciples and for them to be able to recognize him' (civ. 22.19).[28] Yet, rather than dwell on and describe at length the 'brightness' or any new qualities of Christ's body after the resurrection, Augustine often attends to its sameness.[29]

His *Answer to Faustus* draws, to be sure, on such Pauline texts as 1 Cor. 15: 44, 51–2 to affirm the transforming nature of resurrection, with our resurrection directly in mind: 'our flesh will rise, transformed into a spiritual body'; 'this very body will be changed for the better'; 'all things will be made new when this corruptible body puts on incorruption and this mortal body puts on immortality' (c. Faust. 11.3; 11.8).[30]

Christ's risen body, while becoming immortal and 'spiritual', remained the same in the sense that, after the resurrection and up to the ascension, it could be seen by the disciples, touched by them, and

---

[26] *City of God XI–XXII*, 89–90.   [27] Ibid. 91.   [28] Ibid. 532.

[29] Commenting on 1 Cor. 15: 50, 53 in a sermon on the ascension preached in 417, Augustine asks: if 'the flesh will rise again, what does it become? It's changed and becomes a heavenly and angelic body' (s. 264.6; *Sermons* (230–272B), 232). But he is talking here about 'the flesh' of the 'members' of Christ rather than directly about the risen (but not yet ascended) Christ.

[30] *Answer to Faustus*, 117, 122.

recognized by them.[31] In a sermon probably preached in 411, Augustine comments on the invitation to touch him that Jesus made to a group of his disciples and to Thomas—in Luke 24: 39 and John 20: 27, respectively: 'they felt and handled the solidity of his body, since it wasn't enough for some of them to see what they remembered, unless they could also touch what they saw' (s. 361.8).[32] In an earlier sermon, probably to be dated to 403, Augustine interprets John's Gospel to mean that Thomas touched the risen Christ, and Luke's Gospel to mean that the disciples likewise 'saw and touched' him (s. 375C.1–3).[33] In both cases, like many earlier and later commentators,[34] Augustine slips over the fact that neither John nor Luke report that Thomas and the disciples, respectively, took up Jesus' invitation and actually touched him.

---

[31] Augustine understands the risen body to be the same, 'true flesh'. In a sermon preached between 400 and 410, he says 'the Lord Jesus showed his disciples his true flesh in which he had suffered and in which he rose again' (s.229I.1; *Sermons* (184–229Z), 300). In Augustine's stress on the 'true flesh' of the risen Christ, one sees the influence of what Jesus says to his disciples in Lk. 24: 39, 'a ghost does not have flesh and bones as you see that I have'.

[32] Augustine, *Sermons* (341–400), 230. In a sermon preached in either 417 or 418 AD, Augustine likewise argues that the evidence of seeing would not have been enough (s. 229J.1, 3): 'it would have been insufficient to present himself to the eyes for seeing, if he hadn't also offered himself to the hands for touching'. In summary, 'he was seen, he was touched, he ate; it was certainly him' (*Sermons* (184–229Z), 304, 306). In *The City of God*, Augustine similarly claims that, for the disciples to recognize the risen Christ, he 'showed the marks of his wounds for them to touch', and 'even took food and drink' (civ. 22.19; *City of God XI–XXII*, 530). As regards Christ's eating and drinking, we will come to that later. Augustine knows how the Manicheans held that Jesus feigned all the dispositions of a true human life; it was only pretence when he appeared to be hungry, thirsty, sad, happy, and dead (c. Faust. 26.8; 29.2; *Answer to Faustus a Manichean*, 393, 398–9). Opposition to this Manichean error may have encouraged Augustine to stress touching the risen body of Jesus and his 'wounds'. The Manicheans could allege that mere sight deceived the disciples, but they could not explain away touching. It established the truth of the resurrection.

[33] *Sermons* (341–400), 339–41. As Augustine puts it briefly in *De Trinitate*, 'one of his disciples [Thomas] felt his wounds' (4.6; *Trinity*, 157).

[34] See St Ignatius of Antioch, *Epistle to the Smyrnaeans*, 3; *Early Christian Writings: The Apostolic Fathers*, trans. Maxwell Staniforth (Harmondsworth: Penguin, 1968), 119–20.

In this context Augustine considers that Mary Magdalene was told not to touch Christ because she already believed in him: 'The Lord did well to reserve touching him to the incredulous; he forbids this woman [Mary Magdalene] to touch him, because she had already believed in him' (s. 375C.4).[35] Here Augustine, once again with many other commentators, would have been better advised to translate John 20: 17 as 'do not hold on to me' (NRSV) or 'do not cling to me' (REB), rather than 'do not touch me (*noli me tangere*)'. The point at issue is Mary Magdalene's way of relating to Christ rather than the state of the risen body and the possibility of touching it.

Here Augustine passes over in silence the brief story of Mary Magdalene in Matthew 28: 8–10, where she and another Mary accepted the message of an angel of the Lord and seemingly believed in the resurrection *before* they met the risen Jesus, took hold of his feet, and worshipped him. In that episode Jesus did *not* forbid them to keep holding on to his feet, because they already believed in him risen from the dead.

Augustine mitigates his emphasis on touching the body of the risen Christ by observing in a later sermon (preached after 412 AD) that 'Christ is better touched in faith than in the flesh; touching Christ in faith, that is really touching him' (s. 229K.1).[36] A sermon (delivered around the same time) recalls the woman who had suffered for twelve years from an issue of blood (Mk. 5: 24–34): 'the proper way to touch Christ is to touch [him] by faith, like the woman with the issue of blood. Believe like that, and you have touched him' (s. 229L.1).[37]

The invitation to Thomas to touch the wounded hands and side of Jesus (Jn. 20: 27) and to 'the eleven and those who were with them' to touch the hands and feet of Jesus (Lk. 24: 39), as well as the action of Jesus in showing his hands and side to the disciples (Jn. 20: 20), aims at letting the disciples recognize, through their touching and seeing, that 'it is I myself' (Lk. 24: 39), or, in Augustine's terms, verify that it was 'the same body' and that Jesus rose in 'true flesh'. Augustine

---

[35] *Sermons* (341–400), 341. See Anthony Dupont and Ward Depril, 'Marie-Madeleine et Jean 20,17 dans la littérature Patristique', *Augustiniana* 56 (2006), 159–82, at 170–3.
[36] *Sermons* (184–229Z), 309.   [37] Ibid. 313.

acknowledges that we would not expect a risen body to exhibit 'scars (*cicatrices*)'. He insists that Jesus could have 'risen again without his scars', but 'wished to adapt himself' to the disciples and show them 'his scars': 'true flesh' had risen again from death. 'The scars are evidence for this…the hands [of the disciples] touch and feel, to rescue their minds from doubt' (s. 362.12–13).[38]

In a sermon preached during Easter week a few years earlier (probably in AD 403), Augustine had already interpreted the scars as means chosen by Christ to deal with the wounds (*vulnera*) of unbelief in the hearts of those who deny that in his risen state he continues to have 'real flesh':

> It would have been possible, after all, for Christ so to heal the wounds in his flesh that no trace of scars remained; it would have been possible for him not to carry the traces of the nails in his hands and feet, not to carry the trace of the wound in his side; but he permitted those scars to remain *in his flesh*, in order to remove from people's hearts the wound of unbelief, and to take care of their real wounds with the signs and traces of his own wounds.   (s. 375C.2; emphasis added)[39]

'In his flesh' is a key phrase here. Talk of the 'scars' leaves behind any over-spiritualized view of resurrection previously implied or held by Augustine in such early works as *The Soliloquies* (composed in 386–7).[40] The scars demonstrated that the substance of Christ's flesh endured in his risen state. (In parenthesis, one might remark that 'scars' do not fit the picture evoked when Thomas is invited to put his 'hand' into the side of Jesus [Jn. 20:27]. That sounds more like a gaping wound than a superficial scar.)

To establish that Jesus had risen in the true flesh of the same body, Augustine argued that, after the resurrection and before the

---

[38] *Sermons* (341–400), 249–50. See s. 362.14, ibid. 250; ep. 102.7; *Letters 100–155*, 24.

[39] *Sermons* (341–400), 340.

[40] On Augustine's move to a more positive view of the body and a more 'physical' understanding of resurrected bodies, see Hunter, 'Augustine on the Body', in Vessey (ed.), *A Companion to Augustine*, 353–64, at 355–6 and 361–3. In s. 375C.7 (to be dated 403 AD) Augustine ended his sermon by insisting: it was 'true flesh that Truth brought back to life, true flesh that Truth showed to the disciples after the resurrection' (*Sermons* (341–400), 344).

ascension, 'the flesh of our Lord Jesus Christ...maintained human functions, but this was to convince them [the disciples] that it was what had been buried that had also risen again'. The specific 'function' that Augustine intended was eating and drinking. The risen Christ 'ate and drank, not because he was hungry and thirsty'. There was no 'need imposed by decay, requiring the necessity of restoring tissues'. Rather he exercised 'the power of eating...not to supply the needs of his flesh, but to persuade the disciples of the true reality of his body' (s. 362.10, 12).[41]

Augustine had in mind the highpoint of Luke's realistic presentation of the Easter appearances. Let me remind readers of what Augustine read and interpreted in Luke's Gospel and Acts. The risen Jesus asked his disciples for something to eat: 'they gave him a piece of boiled fish, and he took and ate it before them' (Lk. 24: 42–3). Luke echoes this passage twice in the Acts of the Apostles. While 'eating with' the apostles (Acts 1: 4),[42] the risen Jesus commanded them to wait in Jerusalem for the coming of the Holy Spirit. During his meeting in Caesarea with Cornelius, Peter testified to Jesus' resurrection in these terms: 'God raised him on the third day and made him manifest, not to all the people but to us who were chosen by God as witnesses, who ate and drank with him after he rose from the dead' (Acts 10: 40–1).[43] In Luke 24: 43 it is only Jesus who eats, and neither he nor anyone else drinks. In Acts 1: 4 the apostles may also

---

[41] *Sermons* (341–400), 247, 249–50; trans. corrected. As Augustine put matters in his letter to Consentius already quoted (n. 21), 'the power of eating is present, but the need to eat is gone' (ep. 205.4; *Letters 156–210*, 379).

[42] While many translations and commentaries render the *sunalizomenos* of Acts 1: 4 as 'eating with' or 'being at table with', the REB translates 'while he was in their company', and the NRSV translates 'while staying with them', and relegates 'eating' to a note as only a possible translation. On the question of the risen Jesus' 'eating and drinking' with his disciples and how modern exegetes understand this, see G. O'Collins, *Interpreting the Resurrection* (Mahwah, NJ: Paulist Press, 1988), 39–52, 79–82. Here it should be added that Jn. 21: 13 is by no means clear that Jesus himself eats: 'Jesus came and took the bread and gave it to them, and so with the fish'.

[43] This passage underpins Augustine's confident statement: 'Christian faith has no doubt at all with regard to the Saviour himself; even after his resurrection, in his already spiritual but still real flesh, he took food and drink with his disciples' (civ. 13.22; *City of God XI–XXII*, 89).

eat with him, and according to Acts 10: 41 the apostolic witnesses eat and drink with him. We are dealing with the same author, and Luke clearly intends the two passages in Acts (1: 4 and 10: 41) to be understood in the light of what we have already read in Luke 24: 43.

Augustine was aware that, although 'something is always leaving our bodies in a kind of continual flow or current', we 'don't thereby feel our strength deserting us, because we take in more to replace it by eating and drinking'. In other words, 'our strength and energy' are 'recharged' when we are 'at table' (s. 362.11).[44] Augustine was also, of course, perfectly aware that eating and drinking contribute to a 'continual flow or current' of human waste, not to mention growth in weight (and sometimes height) of a given body. But he concentrated on the loss and recharging of 'strength and energy'. In the case of the risen Jesus there was no loss of strength and energy, and so no need of any 'recharging'. He ate and drank only to convince others that he had risen in the true flesh of the same body which had been buried in the tomb. Augustine never raised the questions: did Jesus digest the food and drink that he had ingested? Did he then discharge the waste? Still less did Augustine ask: after the passion and crucifixion had caused Jesus' body to lose weight, did he recover the loss of weight by what he ate after the resurrection?

To lend credibility to the notion of Jesus eating and drinking but not out of any need, Augustine cites the story of Abraham offering hospitality to the Lord, pictured as 'three men' who arrive and eat what Abraham and Sarah put before them (Gen. 18: 1–8). While not called 'angels' in the story, the divine visitors are later identified as angels (Gen. 18: 22; 19:1). Augustine also appeals to the case of Raphael, who acted like a normal man when he accompanied the young Tobias on his journey, brought him safely home again, and finally revealed himself to be 'one of the seven angels who stand ready and enter before the glory of the Lord' (Tob. 12: 15). Augustine claims that in both cases angels 'performed human functions on earth' and really ate. But they did not do so 'out of need' (s. 362.10–11).[45] Hence

---

[44] *Sermons* (341–400), 248.
[45] Ibid. 247–9. See Frederick Van Fleteren, 'Angels', in Fitzgerald (ed.), *Augustine Through the Ages*, 20–2; Emiliano Flori, 'Angels', in Karla Pollmann (ed.), *The*

they offer an analogy to the risen Jesus who, also for 'pastoral' reasons, ate but did not need to do so.

Augustine did not spend much time developing the analogy between Abraham and Sarah's divine visitors eating some cakes, curds, and veal and the risen Jesus eating some fish. He dedicated more space to justifying a comparison with the case of Raphael. For those who read the (Greek) Septuagint, a special difficulty was raised by this text when the angel explains to Tobit and Tobias: 'although you were watching me, I really did not eat or drink anything—but what you saw was a vision' (Tob. 12: 19; NRSV translating the LXX). What Raphael admits here might suggest that, like Raphael, Jesus only seemed to be eating and drinking after his resurrection but did not really do so. The (Latin) text of Tobit that Augustine read made it a little easier, however, to find a parallel between the risen Jesus and what Raphael had done: 'you saw me eating, but you were seeing with your vision' (s. 362.11).[46] This left it open for Augustine to maintain that the risen Jesus really did eat and drink, and thus showed that he had risen in the true flesh of the body.

In Augustine's account, before the ascension Christ appeared and spoke to his disciples, allowed himself to be touched and handled, and ate and drank in order to convince the disciples of his having risen in the same body. At times the risen Christ's eating and drinking seems to count for more with Augustine than Christ's making himself visible, speaking, and allowing himself to be touched: 'he [Christ] spent forty days with them…going in and coming out, eating and drinking; not now because he needed to, but all as an indication of his power, and by way of revealing to them the true reality of his flesh' (s. 262.1).[47] At

---

Oxford Guide to the Reception of Augustine, ii (Oxford: Oxford University Press 2013), 523–7.

[46] *Sermons* (341–400), 247. Elsewhere (civ. 13.22) Augustine cites the same verse (*videbatis me manducare sed visu vestro videbatis*) and for the same purpose—to establish that angels, while having no need to eat, could do so for good reasons. Babcock translates: 'you saw me eat, but it was with your eyes that you saw' (*City of God XI–XXII*, 89). On angels taking food, see also ep. 102.6; *Letters 100–155*, 24.

[47] *Sermons* (230–272B), 217. In a letter written between 406 and 412 AD, Augustine stated: 'after his resurrection Christ showed his scars, not his wounds, to those who doubted, and on account of them he also chose to take food and

other times Augustine points to Christ's allowing himself to be both seen and touched: 'he presented himself to the eyes of his disciples to be seen and to their hands to be touched' (s. 262.1; from 411 AD).[48] All in all, Augustine privileges 'touching' rather than 'seeing' in his account of what the disciples experienced. In the New Testament, however, the language of 'seeing' easily predominates over any touching or hearing. The disciples' decisive experience of the risen Christ is recalled as seeing him.[49] Here what 1 John says, more in general, of their experience has some relevance.[50]

The New Life of Christ: After the Ascension

Preceded by Christ's life and death, his resurrection belongs to a whole sequence of events, distinguished by a 'before' and an 'after'. We have looked at his situation 'after' the resurrection. What of his new state and activities after the ascension? Augustine sums up the impact of the ascension as a *second glorification*. In the course of a sermon preached in 412 AD, he remarks: 'Christ has been twice glorified with respect to the form of the man he took to himself; first, by rising from the dead on the third day; next, by ascending into heaven' (s. 265.8).[51] Such glorification involves, in general, the divine power being

---

drink, not once, but quite often, so that they would not think that it was not a body, but a spirit, and that he appeared to them as something solid, not as imaginary' (ep. 102.7; *Letters 100–155*, 24).

[48] *Sermons* (230–272B), 216.

[49] See G. O'Collins, 'The Appearances of the Risen Christ: A Lexical-exegetical Examination of St Paul and Other Witnesses', *Irish Theological Quarterly* 79 (2014), 128–43, at 136.

[50] In the global statement that opens 1 John (and looks more to the incarnation than the resurrection), 'touching' is mentioned, but 'seeing' predominates: 'We declare to you what was from the beginning, what we have heard, what *we have seen with our eyes, what we have looked at* and touched with our hands, concerning the word of life—this life was *shown* [*to us*] and *we have seen* and testify to it and declare to you the eternal life that was with the Father and *was shown to us*—we declare to you what *we have seen* and heard' (1 Jn. 1: 1–3; emphasis added).

[51] *Sermons* (230–272B), 240.

manifested and final salvation being communicated by the risen and ascended Christ. But what does Augustine say, in particular, about the *post-ascension* existence and activity of Christ?

Here it is relevant to recall something that parallels what was said at the end of the previous section. In the course of a long sermon on the resurrection of the dead from AD 411, Augustine makes a curious comment about the post-resurrection activities of the followers of Christ: 'as for eating and drinking, even though we have the power, we will not be under the necessity of it' (s. 362.12).[52] Later, in *The City of God* Augustine also allows that the resurrected saints will be able to eat, even though there will be no need to do so: 'they will be endowed with the secure and wholly inviolable gift of immortality, and so they will not eat unless they wish to do so; that is, eating will be a possibility but not a necessity for them'. Augustine presses on at once to cite again the example of the three angels eating when they visited Abraham and Sarah, as well as the case of Raphael eating on his journey with Tobias: 'they did not eat because they needed food but because they wanted to, and were able to do so, in order to fit in with human beings by showing human characteristics in pursuing their ministry'. Then Augustine ends by appealing to the risen Jesus himself *before the ascension*: 'in his already spiritual but still real flesh, he took food and drink with his disciples'. While admitting that 'some other more plausible view' might be argued 'with regard to the angels', Augustine sees the same principle verified in the case of the resurrected saints and (before the ascension) the risen Jesus: 'it is not the ability but rather the need to eat and drink that will be removed from such bodies. These bodies will be spiritual…not because they will cease to be bodies but because they will be sustained by a life-giving spirit' (civ. 13.22).[53]

If the resurrected saints can eat provided they want to, what of the risen Jesus *after the ascension*? At the heavenly 'banquet' can he and does he join them in eating? If he maintains this 'human function' (see above) after his resurrection, presumably he does not relinquish it after the ascension, and hence eating could still be an optional activity.

---

[52] *Sermons* (341–400), 249.
[53] *City of God XI–XXII*, 89. In ibid. 22.21, Augustine writes: 'the spiritual flesh will be subject to the spirit, but it will still be flesh, not spirit' (p. 532).

Yet the mature Augustine does not want to insist on this. He warns us against making 'any rash pronouncements', as 'we do not yet have any experience of what the grace of the spiritual body is' (civ. 22.21).[54] If we ask, 'what will the body be like, when it is wholly subject to the spirit and made so fully alive by the spirit that it will need no other nourishment?', Augustine answers cautiously: the risen body (of Christ and his followers) will be 'a spiritual body, having the substance of flesh, of course, but without any carnal corruption' (civ. 22.24).[55]

As regards conjugal relations, Augustine follows Jesus (Matt. 22: 30) in firmly denying that there will be marriage, intercourse, and child-bearing in the resurrection. Nevertheless, God who 'established the two sexes will restore them both', and do so in a way that maintains and enhances the beauty of both. For instance, 'the female organs will still be present' but now 'accommodated to a new beauty' (civ. 22.17).[56] Male 'adornments', such as the 'nipples' on men's chests, will remain in the resurrected body (civ. 22.24).[57] Presumably this will be so in the case of the beautiful, risen body of Jesus. In *Expositions of the Psalms*, when commenting on what Psalm 44 says about the king ('you are the most handsome of men'), Augustine names the risen and ascended Christ as 'beautiful in heaven' (en. Ps. 44.3).[58] But he has just said that Christ was 'beautiful in the womb', 'beautiful in his miracles', and 'beautiful on the cross', and so nothing specific is claimed here about the nature of Christ's heavenly beauty.

Augustine lyrically depicts the life of the resurrected saints, who are fully, perfectly, and definitively happy. In a state of 'complete satisfaction', 'perpetual delight', and 'utterly blissful contemplation and praise of the truth', 'our whole activity will consist of Amen and Alleluia'. Eternal life will consist in 'feasting on' the 'unchangeable divine truth' (s. 362.29–30).[59] In this completely satisfying praise of God, the redeemed will enjoy the closest possible union with their

---

[54] Ibid. 532.   [55] Ibid. 542.

[56] Ibid. 526–7; s. 362.18 likewise cites Matt. 22: 30 to rule out conjugal relations in heaven (*Sermons* (341–400), 254–5).

[57] *City of God XI–XXII*, 540–1; see s. 243.6; *Sermons* (230–272B), 92.

[58] *Expositions of the Psalms* (35–50), trans. Maria Boulding (Hyde Park, NY: New City Press, 2000), 283.

[59] *Sermons* (341–400), 265–6.

The Resurrection of the Crucified Jesus 19

head, as we will see later. Do Augustine's words about the state of 'complete satisfaction' and so forth also implicitly describe the risen Christ himself? In a sermon probably preached in February 404, Augustine says: 'arm in arm with the angels, we shall sing the everlasting hymn "Alleluia". We shall be praising God without ever growing tired' (s. 159B.15).[60] If we praise God 'arm in arm' with the angels, presumably, and even more so, we should be arm in arm with Christ himself in singing God's praise.

Another passage, this time from *The City of God*, raises a similar question. God 'will be the end of our desires; he will be seen without end, loved without satiation, and praised without weariness. And this feeling, this activity, like eternal life itself, will be shared by all' (civ. 22.30).[61] If this activity is shared by all the members of *Totus Christus*, will it be shared by the head?

Augustine was second to none in vividly presenting the final unity of all the redeemed with the risen and ascended Christ, when 'the head and the body form one Christ' (civ. 17.18).[62] He summoned Christians to this future life in Christ: 'be united in him, be one reality, be one person (*in uno estote, unum estote, unus estote*', Io. ev. tr. 12.9).[63] Augustine also expressed the final communion with Christ in terms of praise: 'there we shall praise [the Father]; we shall all be one in [Christ] who is One, oriented towards the One [the Father]; for then, though many, we shall not be scattered (*ibi laudabimus, omnes unus in uno ad unum erimus; quia deinceps multi dispersi non erimus*', en. Ps. 147.28).[64]

In the final kingdom 'that has no end', Augustine expects that 'we shall be still and see, see and love, love and praise' (civ. 22.30).[65] Now, if there will be a profound identity between the ascended Christ and

---

[60] *Newly Discovered Sermons*, trans. Edmund Hill (Hyde Park, NY: New City Press, 1997), 160. Apropos of what Jesus said about resurrection in Matt. 22: 29–30, Augustine remarks: 'what the Lord was promising was not the corruptible life of the flesh, but equality with the angels' (*Expositions of the Psalms* (51–72), trans. Maria Boulding (Hyde Park, NY: New City Press, 2001), 285).

[61] *City of God XI–XXII*, 552.   [62] Ibid. 270.

[63] *Homilies on the Gospel of John*, trans. Edmund Hill (Hyde Park, NY: New City Press, 2009), 236. Here I prefer my own trans., as above.

[64] *Expositions of the Psalms* (121–150), trans. Maria Boulding (Hyde Park, NY: New City Press, 2004), 475; I prefer my own trans., as above.

[65] *City of God XI–XXII*, 554.

his community as they form the whole Christ (*Totus Christus*), what will Christ himself be doing in his glorified humanity? Will he too be 'seeing', 'loving', and 'praising'? In a letter of 417 AD to Claudius Postumus Dardanus, Augustine explained: 'one person is God and man, and the two are the one Jesus Christ, everywhere as God, in heaven as man' (ep. 187.10).[66] Yet even (or should one say especially?) 'in heaven', the divine Word so overshadows the human subjectivity of Christ as man that Augustine seems reluctant to speak of Christ seeing, loving, and praising the Father.

In the *Expositions of the Psalms*, with reference to Christians praying the psalms in this life, Augustine classically expressed their unity of prayer with Christ: 'the one sole Saviour of his body is our Lord Jesus Christ, the Son of God, who prays for us, *prays in us*, and is prayed to by us. He prays for us as our priest, he *prays in us as our head*, and he is prayed to by us as our God. Let us therefore recognize in him our voice and in us his voice' (en. Ps. 85.1; emphasis added).[67] Yet Augustine appears hesitant about describing the heavenly praise of the redeemed as the risen Christ 'praying in us', and as the 'head' of the body making that praise not only 'our voice' but also 'his voice'.

What the Risen Christ Reveals and Does

For Augustine, the two eminent activities of the risen and ascended Christ concern what, as 'head of the body', (a) he reveals to us and (b) what he does for us. In other words, the glorified Christ, now 'in heaven', serves as revealed pledge *and* active instrument of the bodily resurrection of his followers that will come at the last day.

As regards (a), 'he [Christ] *showed* us in the resurrection what we must hope for' (s. 398.9).[68] The rising of Christ from the dead *demonstrated the truth* of our future resurrection and the transformation

---

[66] *Letters 156–210*, 235.

[67] *Expositions of the Psalms* (73–98), trans. Maria Boulding (Hyde Park, NY: New City Press, 2002), 220; trans. adjusted.

[68] *Sermons* (341–400), 450; see s. 233.5, preached in 418: 'What has first occurred in the head will also be given to the members' (*Sermons* (230–272B), 34). Elsewhere (s. 159B.9) Augustine expressed the same point negatively: 'unless our

of our bodies: 'what has been *demonstrated* in advance in the head is to be repeated at the proper time in the members' (s. 362.15; emphasis added).[69] As Augustine puts it in *De Trinitate*, 'we look forward in hope to the realization in Christ's *members*, which is what we are, of what right-minded faith assures us has already been achieved in him as our *head*' (Trin. 2.29; emphasis added).[70]

To highlight the vivid and even passionate nature of this hope, Augustine can leave behind the language of 'head and members' and introduce the image of a bride yearning for her husband.

> It's disgraceful for a married woman not to desire her husband; how much more disgraceful for the Church not to desire Christ! A husband comes to the embraces of the flesh, and is received by his chaste wife with intense longing. The Church's bridegroom is going to come to give us an eternal embrace, to make us his everlasting co-heirs; and we live in such a way, that not only do we not desire his coming, we even dread it. (s. 361.19)[71]

The followers of the risen and ascended Christ should let him stir up their hope of sharing intimately and eternally in his resurrection from the dead.

As regards (b), Augustine sums up the ultimate redemptive impact of the resurrection: 'Christ rose again so that we might rise again' (s. 375B.1).[72] He could 'redeem us from our eternal death because he

---

head had first risen, the other members of the body would not find anything to hope for' (*Newly Discovered Sermons*, 155; a sermon of 404 AD).

[69] *Sermons* (341–400), 252.

[70] *Trinity*, 118. As Augustine put it in a letter to Januarius, 'a resurrection took place in the body of the Lord, so that what the body of the Church hopes for in the end might come first in the head of the Church' (ep. 55.23; *Letters 1–99*, 227). Commenting on Ps. 65, Augustine said: 'as Christians we know that the resurrection of our head has taken place already, and that it will take place in his members. Christ is the head of the Church, and the Church forms his members. What has occurred first in the head will follow in the members. This is our hope' (en. Ps. 65.1; *Expositions of the Psalms* (51–72), 284). More specifically, the 'eternal', resurrected bodies of the members 'will be the sort of body Christ demonstrated in the example of his own resurrection' (civ. 10.29; *City of God I–X*, trans. William Babcock (Hyde Park, NY: New City Press, 2012), 340).

[71] *Sermons* (341–400), 238.   [72] Ibid. 332.

was not only flesh and human soul, but [also] being God and soul and flesh he was the one, only-begotten Son of God'. He could do what no mere human being could do (s. 375B.7).[73] Once they are 'incorporated' into him, his 'members' can 'follow their head in due order' (s. 362.15).[74] They are 'born again', and even here and now their 'new self' is the risen Christ (376A.1),[75] as Augustine teaches in an Easter sermon of 425 AD. In a sermon of the same year on the ascension, he proclaims what will happen to those who have become members of Christ's body: 'where the head has gone on ahead, the body is bound to follow' (s. 395.2).[76]

The followers of Christ have been dead 'in soul' through sin, and are destined to die in the flesh. The death, resurrection, and ascension of Christ form a 'sacrament' (Trin. 4.6; see 4.11),[77] which signifies and effects the hidden, *double reality* of our salvation: the resurrection from sin and then the coming resurrection from the dead—the final state of being 'conformed to the image of the Son of God' (civ. 22.16).[78]

Earlier, in *Homilies on the Gospel of John*, Augustine had spoken of 'two resurrections', that of souls (in the present) and that of bodies (in the future): 'the resurrection of souls is brought about by the eternal and unchanging substance of Father and Son; the resurrection of the bodies, on the other hand, is brought about through the efficacy of the Son's [crucified, risen, and glorious] humanity, which is not co-eternal with the Father' (Io. ev. tr. 23.13).[79] Here Augustine distinguishes what is done through the Son precisely as Son of God from what is done through him precisely as Son of Man: 'God raises souls through Christ the Son of God; through the same Christ, the Son of Man, God raises bodies' (Io. ev. tr. 19.15).[80]

---

[73] Ibid. 337.   [74] Ibid. 252.   [75] Ibid. 348.

[76] Ibid. 432. Eight years earlier, in a sermon on the ascension, Augustine had said: 'the head went before us into heaven. The other members will follow' (s. 264.6; *Sermons* (230–272B), 232–3).

[77] *Trinity*, 156–7, 161.

[78] *City of God XI–XXII*, 525. For a summary of what Augustine says about sin, see James Wetzel, 'Sin', in Fitzgerald (ed.), *Augustine Through the Ages*, 800–2.

[79] *Homilies on the Gospel of John*, 420; these homilies date from around 406 to 421 AD.

[80] Ibid. 350.

The Resurrection of the Crucified Jesus 23

In the first of the two resurrections, 'people pass from the death of infidelity and unbelief to the life of faith, from the death of falsehood to the life of truth, from the death of iniquity to the life of justice. So all this then is also a kind of resurrection from the dead' (Io. ev. tr. 19.8).[81] This first resurrection affects the soul, which receives light and life (Io. ev. tr. 19.12).[82] In the second of the two resurrections, the re-creative power of God will bring about new bodily life through the glorious, risen humanity of Christ: 'the Father' will bring about 'the resurrection of bodies though the Son of Man', who died and rose again (Io. ev. tr. 23.15).[83] At this resurrection (of all human beings) there will be an open, public separation between those raised to the resurrection of life and those raised to that of judgement (Io. ev. tr. 19.18).[84]

Centuries later, Thomas Aquinas would follow Augustine (and Peter Lombard) in teaching that 'Christ's resurrection is the cause of the resurrection of the souls at the present time and of the resurrection of bodies in the future'.[85] Aquinas divided question 56 of the third part of the *Summa theologiae* into two articles which treated Christ's resurrection as the cause, respectively, of the future resurrection of our bodies and of the present resurrection of our souls (or our justification). Christ's own resurrection 'operates instrumentally with a power that is effective not only for the resurrection of the body but also for the resurrection of the soul'. Like Augustine, Aquinas characterized what Christ's resurrection brought as 'newness of life' (q. 56. art. 2 resp., and ad 4).

New Life for Members

'Life' or 'new life' summarizes for Augustine what the crucified, risen, and ascended Jesus communicates to believers: 'Christ is the fountain of life' (s. 233.2)[86] or 'the mediator of life' (Trin. 4.15).[87] By his resurrection and ascension, 'the true mediator of life' has 'called us to new life' (Trin. 4.17).[88] In a sermon preached in 412 or 413,

---

[81] Ibid. 340.   [82] Ibid. 345–6.   [83] Ibid. 422.   [84] Ibid. 354.
[85] Thomas Aquinas, *Summa theologiae*, 3a. q. 56. art. 2 sed contra.
[86] *Sermons* (230–272B), 33.   [87] *Trinity*, 163.
[88] Ibid. 164–5; on Christ as 'the mediator', see also Trin. 4.23; *Trinity*, 390.

Augustine declared: if 'we were death for him', he was and remains 'life for us' (s. 232.5).[89] In fuller terms, 'the resurrection of our Lord Jesus Christ is the new life of those who believe in Jesus. And this is the mysterious meaning of his passion and resurrection...his resurrection is our renewal' (s. 231.2).[90]

If Christ's resurrection from the dead proves the source of our renewal, it is also, as Augustine teaches in a sermon preached after 411 AD, 'the sacrament, the model of the *new life*'. Here Augustine at once quotes Romans 6: 4: 'we have been buried together with Christ through baptism into death, so that just as Christ rose from the dead, in the same way we too may walk in *newness of life*' (s. 229E.3; emphasis added).[91] In an Easter Sunday sermon from 411 or 412, Augustine cites the same verse from Romans and reminds the newly baptized of what Christ has done for them: 'you're *new*; the same old people in bodily appearance, completely *new ones* by the grace of holiness' (s. 229A.1; emphasis added).[92] Through their sharing sacramentally in Christ's death, burial, and resurrection, he has impressed on them new life in the form and likeness of his cross and resurrection.

By means of baptism and confirmation the risen Christ has set his seal or stamp on the neophytes. Augustine reminded those who have been initiated: 'you are his sheep...Read the stamp (*caracterem*) you were sealed with' (s. 229O.3).[93] More often Augustine spoke not of Christ 'branding' people like sheep but of making them 'members' of his body. In an undated sermon preached on some Easter Sunday, Augustine expounded sharing in the Eucharist, the highpoint to which baptism and confirmation led. Receiving 'the body and blood of the priest himself' (the crucified and risen Christ) 'turns' those 'born again of water and the Spirit' into 'members of Christ in the body of Christ' (s. 228B.1, 3).[94]

In a sermon preached in 412 AD, Augustine spoke of the risen Christ 'twice' giving the Holy Spirit: first on the first Easter Sunday (Jn. 20: 22) and after the ascension (at Pentecost) (s. 265.8).[95] He might have

---

[89] *Sermons* (230–272B), 26. [90] Ibid. 19, 20.
[91] *Sermons* (184–229Z), 282. [92] Ibid. 269.
[93] Ibid. 325; in a sermon from 422 AD. [94] Ibid. 261, 262.
[95] *Sermons* (230–272B), 241.

developed this theme and pictured the resurrection and ascension as transforming Christ into the Giver of the Spirit. But Augustine prefers and privileges the language of Christ making members of his body.

The Risen Christ as Minister and Priest

Being 'minister' and 'priest' (or 'mediator') sums up much of Augustine's view of the risen Christ's activity. In opposition to Donatist views that a priest was a true source of holiness rather than simply its visible mediator, Augustine upheld the principle that the risen Christ 'is the only true minister of the sacraments that are administered in his name'.[96] For Augustine, in 'the sacraments of baptism and the Eucharist, the saving work of [the risen] Christ, who is both priest and sacrifice, is actualized for the individual' Christian.[97]

Hence to 're-baptize' anyone already baptized, even by ministers of heretical or schismatic groups, was abhorrent to Augustine. That would mean ignoring the primary role of the risen and ascended Christ in the administration of baptism and the other sacraments. In Augustine's classical statement, whether it is Peter, Paul, Judas, a drunkard, a murderer, or an adulterer who baptizes, it is Christ who baptizes (Io. ev. tr. 5.18; see 6.7).[98]

Reflecting on Psalm 19: 10 ('Lord, save the king'), Augustine recalls the passion of Christ: 'he, who by his suffering gave us an example of how to do battle, may offer our sacrifices also, as our priest risen from the dead and established in heaven.' In short, the risen 'Christ now

---

[96] Gerald Bonner, '*Christus Sacerdos*: The Roots of Augustine's Anti-Donatist Polemic', in Adolar Zumkeller (ed.), *Signum Pietatis*, Festschrift for C. P. Mayer (Würzburg: Augustinus Verlag, 1989), 325–39, at 338.

[97] Ibid. 331. See William Harmless, 'Baptism', in Fitzgerald (ed.), *Augustine Through the Ages*, 84–91. Curiously this encyclopaedia carries no entry on 'priest', 'priesthood', or 'mediator'; the terms do not even appear in the index. Vessey (ed.), *A Companion to Augustine* likewise has nothing to say about Christ as 'priest' or 'mediator'. Yet Daniel J. Jones has shown how central for Augustine were these notions of priest and mediator: *Christus Sacerdos in the Preaching of St Augustine: Christ and Christian Identity* (Frankfurt: Peter Lang, 2004).

[98] *Homilies on the Gospel of John*, 118–19, 127.

offers sacrifice on our behalf' (en. Ps. 19.10).[99] Here the plural, 'our sacrifices', refers to the (singular) Eucharist, just as it does in 'these holy and pure sacrifices (*haec sancta sacrificia illibata*)' of the ancient Roman Canon. It is the one High Priest, the crucified and risen Christ, who now makes the Eucharistic offering for Christians everywhere. It is not the case of many priests offering many sacrifices.

The prayer to 'save the king' led Augustine to consider the role of the crucified and risen high priest in offering the Eucharist—a striking example of the way in which kingly and priestly functions were often intertwined in the scriptures and the Christian tradition. At the time of David, Augustine remarked, 'only kings and priests were anointed; at that time only they were anointed persons. In these two was prefigured the one future king and priest, the one Christ with both functions; and he was given the title "Christ" in virtue of his anointing.' Augustine relates this double role to the present life of Christians as already members of the risen Christ's body: 'not only was our head anointed, his body was too, we ourselves. He is king because he reigns over us and leads us; priest because he intercedes on our behalf' (en. Ps. 26/2.2).[100]

By their baptismal anointing all Christians are incorporated into the risen Christ, *the* anointed priest *and victim*, and become one with him. 'He is like a spotless lamb', Augustine comments,

> who redeemed us by his own spilt blood, uniting us into one body with himself [and] making us his members, so that in him we too are Christ. This is why anointing is proper to all Christians, even though in earlier times under the old covenant it was given to two kinds of persons only. From this it is obvious that we are the body of Christ, being all anointed. In him all of us belong to Christ, but we are Christ too, because in some sense the whole Christ is head and body. (en. Ps. 26/2. 2)[101]

To express this union with the risen Christ through an image of liturgical 'space', Augustine develops what the Letter to the Hebrews says about the Jewish high priest going into the 'secret sanctuary', the Holy of Holies (Heb. 9: 3, 7). Augustine asks:

---

[99] *Expositions of the Psalms* (1–32), trans. Maria Boulding (Hyde Park, NY: New City Press, 2000), 217.
[100] Ibid. 274–5.   [101] Ibid. 275.

What is that [secret, inner room at the heart of the temple]? The place where the high priest alone used to enter [Heb. 9: 3, 7]. But perhaps our high priest is himself the hidden part of God's tabernacle. He received flesh from this tabernacle, and made an inner recess of the tabernacle for us. This was so that others of his members, by believing in him, might be the tabernacle, and he himself be the inner recess. (en. Ps. 26/2. 10)[102]

Obviously this imagery goes beyond anything envisaged by Hebrews. Yet it beautifully evokes the outcome of Christ's sacrifice and the new union it has created: one embodied 'tabernacle' for all the risen Christ's followers, with the exalted high priest himself constituting the 'secret sanctuary', the very Holy of Holies.

Along with the sacrificial theme, Augustine elaborates a *medical* image of the risen Christ's priestly work: 'it was by the divine Physician's humility that mankind was cured from the deadly tumour of pride, which had caused the fall of the first parents...the redemption was nothing else than the neutralization of man's pride by God himself.'[103] The 'humble priest (*sacerdos*)' is simultaneously a 'humble doctor (*medicus*)'. It is the medicine of humble suffering he provides that alone can heal the sickness of human pride. As a humble doctor, Christ encourages us by drinking the medicine first: he 'came to us in our sickness as a doctor. The cup of suffering is bitter, but the doctor drinks it first, in case the sick patient should hesitate to drink it' (s. 299A.5).[104] The risen and ascended Christ, who is eternal priest and sacrificial victim, can also be described by Augustine as our doctor and even our medicine: 'he himself is the doctor, the medico, he himself the medicine...he himself the priest, himself the sacrifice' (s. 374.23).[105] Augustine uses the theme of Christ 'the doctor' and 'the priest' to picture the change brought (by the crucifixion, resurrection, and ascension) from the old covenant to the new: 'all those sacrifices'

---

[102] Ibid. 281.
[103] Rudolphus Arbesmann, 'The Concept of "Christus Medicus" in St. Augustine', *Traditio* 10 (1954), 1–28, at 9. In well over forty texts Augustine develops or at least alludes to the healing activity of Christ, the crucified and risen, divine physician; see ibid. 2–3.
[104] *Newly Discovered Sermons*, 268.   [105] Ibid. 407.

were 'done away with' and 'one sacrifice' was provided—'the body of Christ purging away sins' (s. 374.19).[106]

Drawing on Ephesians, Augustine uses the language of 'head' in a priestly way: 'he himself [Christ], you see, is the head of the Church [Eph. 5: 23], the One who has already ascended into heaven and is seated at the right hand of the Father, showing us in his whole burnt offering of himself what we should also be hoping for where our flesh is concerned' (s. 198.44).[107] This is a self-offering of the risen Christ *and his members*: 'he will take with him the body whose head he is and offer it as his kingdom to God' (Io. ev. tr. 19.18).[108]

The image of *head and body* allows Augustine to picture a priesthood now shared by the entire Church: 'it is the whole universal Church which is the body of that one priest. To the priest belongs his body. That, after all, is why the Apostle Peter says to the Church itself, "a holy people, a royal priesthood" [1 Pet. 2: 9]' (s. 198.49).[109] This 'fellowship of the saints is offered to God as a universal sacrifice through the great priest'. 'In his passion' he 'offered himself for us… that we might be the body of such a great head' (civ. 10.6).[110] The crucified and risen Christ has made those for whom his sacrifice was offered one with himself in his priestly, sacrificial role.

Conclusions

In an early sermon on the ascension (from 396–7 AD), Augustine held together what came 'before' and what came 'after': from Christ's conception, life, death, descent to the dead, resurrection, and ascension, to his sitting at the right hand of God in heaven. He told his congregation: 'after rising again, you see, he ascended into heaven in the same body in which, after dying, he had visited the underworld. He now, that is, deposited in heaven that dwelling of his [now]

---

[106] Ibid. 403. In s. 198.51 (a very long sermon from 404 AD), Augustine speaks of the head of the Church purging away sins: 'the one and only priest is the mediator himself, the sinless head of the Church, through whom is effected the purging away of our sins' (ibid. 220).

[107] Ibid. 213.   [108] *Homilies on the Gospel of John*, 354.
[109] *Newly Discovered Sermons*, 218.   [110] *The City of God I–X*, 311.

immortal flesh, which he had fashioned for himself in the womb of his virgin mother' (s. 265B.1).[111] The resurrection of Christ, as Augustine persistently emphasized, maintained 'the same body', even if it had become 'immortal flesh'.

In spelling out the details of the 'immortal flesh' that is Christ's 'same body' in his resurrection, we have drawn from many works of Augustine: his *Expositions of the Psalms*, *De Trinitate*, *Sermons*, *Answer to Faustus a Manichean*, *Letters*, *City of God*, and *Homilies on the Gospel of John*. The works are listed here in the order in which they were first quoted in this chapter. Inevitably it made most use of Augustine's *Sermons*, which treat the resurrection of Christ repeatedly and at length when expounding the liturgical seasons of Easter and the Ascension. In any case, the *Sermons* offer the largest source; their eleven volumes, even without the *Homilies on the Gospel of John*, make them the most extensive section in *The Works of Saint Augustine* published by New City Press.[112] Seven major themes have emerged from examining Augustine's account of the resurrection of Christ himself.

First, Augustine highlighted belief in the resurrection of Jesus as the heart of Christian faith. It is this belief that identifies and defines the members of the Church.

Second, he consistently expressed the resurrection in terms of Christ's own active and divine role: 'he could raise his own flesh' (s. 232.2).[113] Here he followed the Gospel of John rather than the letters of Paul. The apostle regularly fell into line with early Christian usage by portraying the resurrection as God the Father's action through the Holy Spirit on the dead Jesus: 'God raised Jesus from the dead' (Rom. 10: 9). But Augustine preferred to underline the divine power of Christ and say: 'Jesus is risen from the dead', or 'Jesus rose from the dead'.

Third, Augustine picks up the language deployed by Paul in 1 Corinthians 15, and speaks of Christ's risen existence as 'spiritual'

---

[111] *Sermons* (230–272B), 249.

[112] John E. Rotelle et al. (eds.), 39 vols. (Hyde Park, NY: New City Press, 1991–2013). For a general study of Augustine's preaching, see Hildegund Müller, 'Preacher: Augustine and His Congregation', in Vessey (ed.), *A Companion to Augustine*, 297–309.

[113] *Sermons* (230–272B), 24; this sermon dates from 412 or 413 AD.

and immortal. But he also insists on the risen body as retaining 'the substance of flesh'. It enjoys a new 'brightness', but this luminous quality is 'hidden' from the disciples, when they see and touch 'real' flesh. Christ himself can eat and drink, even though he does not now need to do so. Despite the weight of the New Testament witness, Augustine privileges 'touching' rather than seeing the risen Christ as the decisive post-resurrection experience that enables the disciples to recognize him.

Fourth, while constituting a further 'glorification' of the risen Christ who is 'beautiful in heaven', the ascension does not seem to end his power to eat and drink, even though, like the resurrected saints, he is under no necessity to do so. Augustine, in a memorable passage from the *Expositions of the Psalms*, speaks of Christ who 'prays in us as our head'. Yet he remains reluctant to state clearly that the heavenly Christ, united with his resurrected members and definitively making with them the one *Totus Christus*, will share in their perpetual delight and sing with them the divine praises.

Fifth, the resurrection and ascension reveal what 'we must hope for'. The risen Christ constitutes the pledge of coming resurrection for his members. He is also the 'sacrament' that signifies and effects their resurrection from the death of sin and their future resurrection from physical death. He is the instrument of our 'double' resurrection.

Hence, sixth, the risen and ascended Christ is the *mediator of new life*. He renews and mediates new, eternal life to those who have become members of his body through baptism, confirmation, and the Eucharist.

Seventh, the risen Christ is the 'only true minister of the sacraments administered in his name'. The invisible but effective minister of baptism, he is also the priest who eternally 'offers sacrifice on our behalf'. He is not only the priest who 'intercedes on our behalf' but also the humble priest and doctor who 'purges away sins'.

Ultimately, what Augustine preached and wrote about the resurrection of Christ illustrates a clear preference for *Christus pro nobis* over *Christus in se*, 'Christ for us' (the last three themes) rather than 'Christ in himself' (the first four themes). Augustine insisted that 'the faith of Christians is in the resurrection of Christ'. But what caught Augustine's attention was all that the resurrection promises us and does for us—the risen Christ as the pledge and cause of our final salvation.

The Resurrection of the Crucified Jesus 31

That was the engine driving Augustine's preaching and writing about the resurrection of Christ. He offered more material on the last three themes than on the first four themes.

Augustine's commitment and passion loomed large when he addressed the Easter mystery. In a sermon from 396 or 397 AD, he remarked: 'we didn't see him hanging on the cross, nor observe him rising from the tomb. We hold on to all of this by faith, we behold it with the eyes of the heart' (s. 263.3).[114] Twenty years later he spoke of 'an inner gazing of the heart' (s. 264.2).[115] He could have been speaking about himself. His works repeatedly illustrated his own 'inner gazing of the heart' directed at Christ gloriously risen from the dead, the head of the body in whom Augustine had come to believe 'with the eyes of his heart'.

---

[114] *Sermons* (230–272B), 220. On believing as seeing Christ risen, see ep. 147.9–11; *Letters 100–155*, 323–4.

[115] *Sermons* (230–272B), 227. On the Lord 'offering himself to the eyes of the heart', see en. Ps. 26/2.15; *Expositions of the Psalms* (1–32), 284.

2
Arguments for Jesus' Resurrection
Augustine's Rhetoric

'One who tries to speak not only wisely but also eloquently', Augustine wrote in *De Doctrina Christiana* (*On Teaching Christianity*), 'will surely be of more use if he can do both' (doctr. Chr. 4.5.8). What enabled Augustine to speak wisely was the truth he found chiefly in the inspired Scriptures (doctr. Chr. 4.5.7). In fact, he found both wisdom and eloquence in those Scriptures: 'where I understand these [biblical] authors, it seems to me that not only could there be nothing wiser, but also nothing more eloquent than the sacred writers' (doctr. Chr. 4.6.9). Augustine's rhetoric combined both wisdom and eloquence, including eloquent precision (doctr. Chr. 4.14.30–1).[1]

Augustine's preaching and writing expressed his response to the salvation that he experienced through the incarnation, death, resurrection, and ascension of Christ, along with the gift of the Holy Spirit. Augustine's rhetorical skills served to integrate what he had received and argue for it forcibly. His powerful rhetoric enhanced his performance as preacher and author who served the Church.

Through his study of rhetoric, Augustine had learned how to identify issues, construct arguments, and compose speeches. He knew how to instruct, inspire, and convince audiences, and did so by appealing to their imaginations and emotions. As a Christian he set himself to seek wisdom, pursue truth, and win over audiences to accept and practise fully the Christian message.

---

[1] *Teaching Christianity*, trans. Edmund Hill (Hyde Park, NY: New City Press, 1996), 204, 205, 209.

Rhetorical Wisdom and Eloquence

The preface to this book drew attention to the way in which Augustine's skills as a rhetorician helped to shape what he said and wrote about the resurrection of Jesus Christ. Here as elsewhere, Augustine set himself to clarify issues, define terms, develop arguments, highlight telling details, and engage the attention of his hearers or readers. The Gospels, the letters of Paul, and other scriptural sources fed his treatment of the Lord's resurrection, and made that treatment an extensive biblical commentary. Hence his ability to understand and explain the texts of Sacred Scripture formed and fashioned, from beginning to end, what he wished to say about Christ's rising from the dead. He constantly brought his rhetorical eloquence to bear on the inspired wisdom of the Scriptures.[2]

Augustine remained rhetorically sensitive to the capacity and interests of various audiences. Thus, in dealing with an objection persisting until modern times that dwells on contradictions between the Gospel accounts of the resurrection, Augustine remarked: 'to show that all four evangelists never contradict each other on points that they all talk about' would be 'an extremely laborious task'. He added: 'if I were to show you how this is…the majority of listeners would be overwhelmed with boredom long before they could be brought relief by the knowledge of the truth' (s. 240.1).[3] Augustine did not specify the 'points that they [the evangelists] all talk about', but they could easily be listed: a 'third-day' resurrection of Christ after his death and burial, the prominence of women among the Easter witnesses, the discovery of

---

[2] For contemporary research into Augustine's scriptural hermeneutics, see Joseph T. Kelley, *What Are They Saying About Augustine?* (Mahwah, NJ: Paulist Press, 2014), 123–6; Karla Pollmann, 'Hermeneutical Presuppositions', in Allan D. Fitzgerald (ed.), *Augustine Through the Ages: An Encyclopedia* (Grand Rapids, MI: Eerdmans, 1999), 426–9. On Augustine and rhetoric, see Nello Cipriani, 'Rhetoric', ibid. 724–6; Hanne Roer, 'Rhetoric', in K. Pollmann (ed.), *The Oxford Guide to the Historical Reception of Augustine*, iii (Oxford: Oxford University Press, 2013), 1650–7; R. S. O. Tomlin, '*Spes Saeculi*: Augustine's Worldly Ambition and Career', in Mark Vessey (ed.), *A Companion to Augustine* (Oxford: Wiley-Blackwell, 2012), 57–68.

[3] *Sermons* (230–272B), trans. Edmund Hill (New Rochelle, NY: New City Press, 1993), 65.

the empty tomb, the role of the (eleven) male disciples headed by Peter, and so forth. Nowadays we would prefer to speak of the New Testament authors converging on *primary* points and differing in their accounts on *secondary* details (e.g. Luke's special story about the two disciples who walk to Emmaus).[4] But the basic response to a recurrent objection remains similar.

Augustine brings up this objection in the course of three sermons (s. 240–2) which he preached on consecutive days during the Easter season.[5] In these sermons he set himself to refute the errors of pagan philosophers who ruled out the very possibility of resurrection: above all, Pythagoras, Plato, the Neoplatonists, and Stoic pantheists. They could differ by maintaining either no life at all after death (the Epicureans), reincarnation for the souls of those who needed further purification and immortal, bodiless bliss for the souls of the virtuous (Plato and Neoplatonists), or individual souls disappearing at death into the seminal reason of the universe (Stoics). But they all agreed in making no room for a bodily resurrection of the dead. In particular, against the views of Plotinus and (his disciple) Porphyry (Neoplatonists of the late third century AD who rejected the resurrection of Jesus),[6] Augustine not only put an eloquent case for God raising the dead to a new, eternal existence for body and soul, but also dealt with some objections against this belief.

These objections included items that we aired in the first chapter: Christ (a) eating after his resurrection, and (b) rising 'with the scars of his wounds'. If 'the body's liability to decay is not going to rise again, why did the Lord Jesus eat?' Augustine's response is pithy and rhetorically effective: 'that he ate was a matter of his power, not of his need'. Two alternatives lay the objection to rest: 'if he had had a craving to eat, he would have been in need…if he hadn't been able to eat, it would have meant he had less capability'. For good measure,

---

[4] See G. O'Collins, *Believing in the Resurrection: The Meaning and Promise of the Risen Jesus* (Mahwah, NJ: Paulist Press, 2012), 61–2.

[5] *Sermons* (230–272B), 65–84.

[6] In civ. 10.28–9 (*The City of God I–X*, trans. William Babcock (Hyde Park, NY: New City Press, 2012), 337–41), and civ. 22.25–8 (*The City of God XI–XXII*, trans. William Babcock (Hyde Park, NY: New City Press, 2013), 542–6), Augustine discusses at length a lost work of Porphyry, *On the Return of the Soul*.

Augustine throws in a reference to stories from the Old Testament (e.g. the visit of angels to Abraham and Sarah in Gen. 18: 1–9), which we saw him discuss at greater length in Chapter 1: 'Did even angels fail to eat, when they were given hospitality by our ancestors, and yet they were not liable to decay?'[7] Here again, immortal, incorruptible existence did not rule out the capacity to eat, exercised by angels for 'pastoral' reasons.

Augustine also raises a question about an alleged defect in the risen body of Christ as pictured in the Easter stories of Luke and John: 'why did the Lord rise again with the scars of his wounds?' Once again Augustine argues that 'this too was a matter of power, not of need. He wished to rise like that', for 'he wished to present himself like that to some people who had doubts. The scars of the wounds in that flesh healed the wounds of unbelief.'[8] Augustine translates to the level of terse and compelling rhetoric a detail in the resurrection narratives.

Sermons 240, 241, and 242 were directed explicitly 'against the pagans'. An eloquent rhetoric fuelled and fashioned Augustine's 'apology' for Christ's resurrection. The same holds true of the case he developed elsewhere for this central Christian belief: in further sermons, *Answer to Faustus a Manichean*, *The City of God*, *The Trinity*, and other works.

In a fourfold, rhetorical apology, (1) Augustine insisted that belief in the resurrection of Jesus Christ establishes the identity and defines the faith of Christians, and hence is supremely important. In justifying this belief in resurrection, he appealed to (2) the divine power shown in creation, along with further evidence from created nature, to (3) evidence from the historical rise of Christianity, which without the adequate cause of Christ's resurrection would remain an unexplained effect, and to (4) the desires of those whom he addressed—above all, their deep hunger for lasting happiness. In the course of all this, as we shall see, he remained clear about the issue at stake, mustered evidence from the Scriptures and human experience, and skilfully appealed to the emotions of his audience. Those feelings also entered the cumulative case Augustine rhetorically constructed.

---

[7] *Sermons* (230–272B), 79.   [8] Ibid.

The Central Issue

In the second of his three sermons 'against the pagans', Augustine stated laconically: 'the resurrection of the dead is the special belief of Christians' (s. 241.1).[9] He did not tolerate any lack of clarity about the point at issue, frequently insisting that belief in the resurrection of Jesus Christ establishes the faith and identity of Christians. In a sermon preached during the Easter octave of 418 AD, for example, he exhorted the congregation: 'Let us believe in Christ crucified, but in him who rose again on the third day. That's the faith which... distinguishes us from the pagans, distinguishes us from the Jews; the faith by which we believe that Christ has risen from the dead' (s. 234.3).[10] In a sermon preached a few years earlier he had stated: 'the resurrection of the Lord Jesus Christ is the distinctive mark (*forma*) of the Christian faith...both friends and enemies have believed that Christ was crucified and died; that he rose again, only his friends have known.' Hence Augustine concluded: 'this is what defines our faith, the resurrection of the Lord Jesus Christ' (s. 229H1, 3).[11]

Not only Augustine's sermons but also his frankly apologetical works feature this conviction. In a treatise written between 408 and 410 AD against Faustus, a Manichean, he observed: 'Even the pagans, to be sure, believe that Christ died, but the faith proper to Christians is that he rose' (c. Faust. 16.29).[12]

But why should non-believers come to accept this belief and accept it as centrally important? What could explain and justify belief in the resurrection of Jesus either for outsiders or for Christians wavering in their Easter faith? What kind of rhetorical 'apology' did Augustine develop to legitimate the 'distinctive mark of Christian faith'? First of

---

[9] Ibid. 70. This recalls the memorable statement with which Tertullian (d. around 225) opened his *De Resurrectione Carnis* (On the resurrection of the flesh): 'fiducia Christianorum resurrectio mortuorum, illam credentes hoc sumus (the resurrection of the dead constitutes the confidence of Christians. By believing it, we are what we claim to be)'; trans. mine.

[10] *Sermons* (230–272B), 37.

[11] *Sermons* (184–229Z), trans. Edmund Hill (New Rochelle, NY: New City Press, 1993), 295, 297.

[12] *Answer to Faustus a Manichean*, trans. Roland J. Teske (Hyde Park, NY: New City Press, 2007), 222.

all, he appealed repeatedly to creation and evidence from created nature.

Creation and the Created World

Background beliefs and theories often prove decisive when facing the resurrection of Jesus and the hope for general resurrection.[13] In this context Augustine's 'prior' faith in God as Creator, almost inevitably, proves essential for his argument. 'The Creator who made all things from nothing', Augustine maintains, will not 'lack the means' when it comes to the work of resurrection (civ. 22.13).[14] Since in his 'wisdom and compassion' God 'created what was not', he is also able to 'free what he created from corruption' (civ. 22.27).[15] Through his 'omnipotence' the Creator can 'revive' and 'restore' the dead to life (civ. 22.20).[16]

Rhetorically addressing a pagan who denies the resurrection, Augustine says: 'the one whom you believe to be God Almighty, that is the One who I say raises the dead. If you say, "it [the resurrection] can't happen", you are detracting from the Almighty. But if you believe he really is almighty, why do you brush me aside when I say this?' (s. 240.2).[17]

In the same series of three sermons (240–2), Augustine imagines again a pagan audience and, referring to the power of God endorsed by the *Timaeus* of Plato, sharpens this paradox of the resurrection. By raising the dead, the almighty God does what is seemingly impossible: '"But it's impossible", they say, "for an earthy body to be in heaven". What if God so wishes? Answer against God and say, "God can't do it". Don't you too, pagan though you are, say that God is all-powerful?' Hence 'God, who can even do what is impossible, brought

---

[13] See G. O'Collins, *Easter Faith: Believing in the Risen Jesus* (London: Darton, Longman and Todd, 2003), 1–24.

[14] *City of God XI–XXII*, 525.   [15] Ibid. 526.

[16] Ibid. 530; on Augustine's belief in God as creator, see Rowan Williams, 'Creation', in Fitzgerald (ed.), *Augustine Through the Ages*, 251–4. Vessey (ed.), *A Companion to Augustine* includes a chapter on redemption (Lewis Ayres, 416–27), but none on creation.

[17] *Sermons* (230–272B), 66.

everything back to his will. I mean what else does "you cannot be immortal, but I will ensure that you will never die" amount to, but "I can even do what cannot possibly be done?"' (s. 242).[18]

Moving beyond this general presupposition, Augustine elsewhere points specifically to 'the miracle' of the world and all the marvels we observe in it. Apropos of the resurrection not only of Christ but also of others, he asks: 'Why, then, would God not have the power to make the bodies of the dead rise again? He is the one who created a world full of *innumerable marvels* in the heavens, on earth, in the air, and in the waters; and of course the world itself is without doubt a greater and more outstanding *miracle* than all the *wonders* with which it is filled' (civ. 21.7; emphasis added).[19] The wonders *in* the world and the wonder that *is* the whole created world, 'itself a unique *miracle* and the greatest of them all' (civ. 21.9; emphasis added),[20] encourage Augustine to accept that God can raise the dead and, in fact, has raised the crucified Jesus.

In the third of his sermons 'against pagans' who deny the resurrection, Augustine refers to what he considers a greater miracle, that of babies being born each day: 'it is in fact a greater miracle, so many people being born each day who didn't previously exist, than a few who having risen again, who did exist. And yet this kind of miracle is not seriously considered and appreciated, but being so common is disregarded as uninteresting' (s. 242.1).[21] Augustine is more astonished by the miracle of that which did not exist coming into existence (birth) than by the miracle of that which once existed being restored in a new existence (resurrection).

In another sermon (preached around 411 AD), Augustine puts the same argument more vividly by linking (a) our being fashioned in our

---

[18] Ibid. 81. [19] *City of God XI–XXII*, 457.

[20] Ibid. 464. See also civ. 22.24 (ibid. 541) where Augustine enthusiastically rejoices in the beauty of created nature. Later we will come to physical miracles (such as healings) to which Augustine appeals. But here he uses 'miracle' in the broader sense, as that which excites wonder; for Augustine creation is *the great* miracle, since it reflects the very creative nature of God. A little surprisingly there is no entry 'Miracle' in Fitzgerald (ed.), *Augustine Through the Ages*; even more surprisingly, 'miracle' does not feature in the index, as is also the case with Vessey (ed.), *A Companion to Augustine*.

[21] *Sermons* (230–272B), 78.

mother's womb with (b) the tomb from which Christ himself rose and others will rise. He waxes eloquent about the wonderful miracle of what God does in forming us before birth. God, who brings us forth 'in proper shape from the womb', can also bring us alive 'from the tomb'. Augustine calls human beings taking shape in their mothers' wombs 'a daily miracle'. He regrets that 'it's so excessively common' that 'it has lost its power to strike the wonder' which Augustine himself feels and which fuels the womb/tomb argument (s. 242A.2).[22]

Many people today, to be sure, do not share Augustine's astonishment at the marvellous universe in which we live. Yet there are also many who find themselves amazed at what modern cosmology, physics, chemistry, biology, and medicine (e.g. the intra-uterine development of babies) have revealed about the workings of nature. Astonishment at the wonders of God's *creation* might well predispose them to accept the Christian belief in the *new creation* that is Christ's resurrection and will be ours.

As a skilful rhetorician, Augustine introduces specific analogies from the natural world that can lend plausibility to belief in the resurrection of Christ and the general resurrection to come. 'The whole of creation speaks of resurrection', he says in a sermon from 411 AD: each day, for instance, waking follows sleeping, and each year the leaves on trees return (s. 361.10).[23]

Some of Augustine's predecessors had already developed this analogy. To strengthen hope in our coming resurrection Clement of Rome, for example, noted some 'processes of resurrection going on' all the time in nature: the succession of day and night, and the crops which come into being from the seed that 'decays' in the earth

---

[22] Ibid. 86.
[23] *Sermons* (341–400), trans. Edmund Hill (New Rochelle, NY: New City Press, 1995), 231. Augustine would have delighted in modern scientific insights into the phenomenon of dying and rising or being reborn, of which Ian Bradley has written: 'scientists, particularly biochemists and biologists, are increasingly finding and demonstrating the extent to which life at all levels is dependent on death. An important dimension of this discovery is the phenomenon known as programmed cell death through which the healthy growth and development of all living creatures depends on cells constantly dying and being reborn' ('Sacrifice', in Adrian Hastings, Alistair Mason, and Hugh Pyper (eds.), *The Oxford Companion to Christian Thought* (Oxford: Oxford University Press, 2000), 637–9, at 638).

(*1 Clement*, 24).[24] Tertullian appealed to the divine power shown in the change of seasons, the return of daylight after the darkness of the night, and the 'greater fruitfulness' of seeds 'when they have rotted and are destroyed' (*De Resurrectione*, 12; trans. mine). He concluded that 'all things are preserved by dying. All things, from their destruction, are restored' (*Apologeticum*, 48.8).[25] For these, Augustine, and other ancient Christian authors, the pattern of 'new life after death' found in the natural world hints at the resurrected life that has already come to Jesus after his death and burial, and will come to others.

All those who read or hear the New Testament will be already familiar with the picture of grain that 'dies' in the earth and gives rise to fertile, new life (Jn. 12: 23–4; 1 Cor. 15: 37–8). At Easter many worshippers sing a hymn set to a French carol melody by John MacLeod Campbell Crum (1872–1958): 'Now the green blade riseth, from the buried grain, | Wheat that in the dark earth many days has lain. | Love lives again, that with the dead has been. | Love is come again, like wheat that springeth green.'

When replying to objections against the resurrection, Augustine takes up the union of soul and body, where 'nature' allows something 'incorporeal to be bound by a corporeal tie'. In a wonderful way souls are joined to 'earthly bodies' and 'give them life'. This allows Augustine the rhetorician to argue *a fortiori*: 'if the soul, which is more exalted than any body' can 'be bound to an earthly body, what keeps an earthly body from being elevated to a heavenly body by the will of the same God who made this living being?' Thus Augustine's anthropology enables him to press the question: 'Why is it that we are not much more astounded and amazed that incorporeal souls…are bound to bodies than we are that our bodies, though earthly, should be elevated to abodes which, though heavenly, are nevertheless corporeal?' In other words, why do we fail to recognize (a) the union of soul and body as more marvellous than (b) the heavenly transformation of our earthly body that resurrection involves?

---

[24] *Early Christian Writings: The Apostolic Fathers*, trans. Maxwell Staniforth (London: Penguin Books, 1968), 36.

[25] Tertullian, *Apology*, trans. Emily Joseph Daly (Washington, DC: Catholic University of America Press, 1950), 119.

Augustine finds an explanation in the dulling effect of constant experience:

> The explanation can only be that we see the former [a] all the time—it is in fact what we are—but we are not yet the latter [b] and have never seen it all. If we consult sober reason, however, we shall surely find that it is a more wondrous divine work to interweave corporeal and incorporeal things in some way than it is to link heavenly and earthly things which, although different, are nevertheless both corporeal. (civ. 22.4)[26]

Endorsing the force of this argument, from (a) a greater wonder (the union of soul and body that is the human condition) to (b) a lesser wonder (the heavenly transformation entailed by resurrection), obviously depends on accepting Augustine's anthropology. His line of argument belongs within a 'background theory' of creation and, in particular, of the created nature of human beings that can lend credibility to resurrection belief. It also presupposes accepting that, while 'different', 'heavenly and earthly things are nevertheless both spiritual', and in some sense 'corporeal'.

Human History: The 'Contemptible' Witness

If nature makes resurrection believable, so too does human history. Augustine argues from the visible *effect* which his readers could see for themselves (almost the whole of Roman society by that time accepting the resurrection of Jesus) to the *only adequate cause* for this historical phenomenon, Christ's victory over death. Since the original witnesses to that resurrection were ill equipped, the success of their message of Christ's resurrection cannot be explained on merely human grounds. God must have worked in and through these witnesses and established the truth of their message.

Thus unless one accepts the resurrection, one cannot, Augustine claims, account for an 'incredible' historical fact: 'a few fishermen out

---

[26] *City of God XI–XXII*, 499–500. On the 'wonderful' union of body and soul, Augustine had written earlier: 'the body is united with the soul to make a whole and complete human being. And if this were not so utterly commonplace, it would plainly be even more incredible' (civ. 10.29; *City of God I–X*, 339). See also Roland J. Teske, 'Soul', in Fitzgerald (ed.), *Augustine Through the Ages*, 807–12.

on the sea of this world with the nets of faith, with no education in the liberal arts, completely untaught in the doctrines of pagan thought, not trained in *grammar*, nor equipped with *dialectic*, nor swollen with *rhetoric*', could manage to catch 'all those fish of every kind and even—more wonderful still, because more rare—some of the philosophers themselves'. In short, 'a few obscure men, of no standing and of no education, were so effective in persuading the world, including the learned, of something so incredible'—namely, 'that Christ rose in the flesh and ascended with his flesh into heaven' (civ. 22.5).[27]

Augustine names here the first three of the liberal disciplines which were so highly valued in the Roman world and at which he himself excelled (grammar, dialectic, and rhetoric). He does this to highlight the uneducated state of the first witnesses to the resurrection. How could such nobodies overcome this major obstacle blocking the success of their message of the resurrection? 'If many noble, eminent, and learned people', Augustine argues, 'had reported that they *saw* this [the resurrection and ascension of Christ] happen', it 'would be no wonder that the world believed them; in fact it would be perverse to refuse to believe witnesses such as these'. But what 'if—and this is the truth of the matter— the world believed a few obscure men of no importance and no learning who reported in speech and writing what they had *seen*'? Their proclamation of the resurrection is all the more believable for having prevailed despite such massive difficulties.

The *means* (a 'tiny number of obscure, unimportant, unlearned men') are not, from a human point of view, proportionate to the *effect*: 'the resurrection of Christ and his ascension into heaven with the flesh

---

[27] *City of God XI–XXII*, 500–1; emphasis added. Augustine's argument echoes and develops the reaction of the Sanhedrin to Peter and John's bold proclamation of Jesus' resurrection: 'they realized that they were uneducated and ordinary men' (Acts 4: 13). Augustine ignores such educated early Christians as Paul and Luke to concentrate on those whom we know to have been fishermen: Peter, James, and John. His reference to 'all those fish of every kind' may echo a scene in which Peter and 'the sons of Zebedee' (Jn. 21: 2) feature: the astonishing catch of 153 great fish (Jn. 21: 11), which could symbolize the Church coming to include in one unbroken net people of all kinds. Or it may echo a parable of the kingdom in which a net thrown into the sea gathers fish 'of every kind' (Matt. 13: 47). On possible symbolic meanings for the 153 fish, see Raymond E. Brown, *The Gospel According to John* (xiii–xxi) (New York: Doubleday, 1970), 174–5.

in which he rose again' being 'believed the whole world over'. It can only be 'divinity' that 'has made itself even more *miraculously* convincing by using such contemptible witnesses'. 'Miraculously' will introduce a new theme in the argument that Augustine addresses to those who continue to reject the resurrection of Christ, 'those few who remain so persistent and obstinate in not believing what the whole world now believes' (civ. 22.5).[28] But before moving to the new theme (and two items missing in Augustine's argument), let me make four comments on what he has so far argued.

(a) First, I added emphasis above to 'saw' and 'seen' to bring out how Augustine relies in this passage from *The City of God* on eyewitnesses' testimony to the risen Christ.[29] Sometimes he talks of Christ being heard and touched as well as seen by the disciples: 'he didn't speak only in words to their ears, but also in appearance to their eyes, and not content with presenting himself to their sight, he also offered himself to be handled and felt' (s. 242.1, with reference to Lk. 24: 36–40).[30]

Elsewhere Augustine seems to privilege touching the risen Christ rather than seeing the risen Christ, as we have seen in the first chapter. In a sermon probably preached in 411 AD, he comments on the invitation to touch him that Jesus made to a group of his disciples and to Thomas—in Luke 24: 39 and John 20: 27, respectively: 'they felt and handled the solidity of his body, since it wasn't enough for some of them to see what they remembered, unless they could also touch what they saw' (s. 361.8).[31] In a sermon preached in either 417 or 418 AD, Augustine likewise argues that the evidence of seeing would not have been enough: 'it would have been insufficient to present himself to the eyes for seeing, if he hadn't also offered himself to the

---

[28] *City of God XI–XXII*, 501; emphasis added.

[29] The New Testament, while twice picturing the disciples as seeing the ascension (Lk. 24: 50–1; Acts 1: 6–11), never alleges that anyone literally saw the event of the resurrection itself. Augustine's language about the first Christian witnesses having 'seen' the resurrection is shorthand for their having seen the risen Christ when, after the resurrection, he took the initiative of 'appearing' to them or letting them see him.

[30] *Sermons* (230–272B), 78.   [31] *Sermons* (341–400), 230.

hands for touching' (s. 229J.1).[32] In one passage of *The City of God* Augustine states simply that, for the disciples to recognize him, the risen Christ 'showed the marks of the wounds for them to touch' (civ. 22.19).[33] Like many earlier and later commentators, Augustine slips over the fact that neither John nor Luke report that Thomas and the other disciples, respectively, took up Jesus' invitation and actually touched him. In any case, where Augustine privileges touching over seeing the risen Christ, he shows himself at odds with the New Testament witness. There the disciples' decisive experience of the risen Christ is presented as *seeing him*. The language of seeing clearly predominates over any touching and, for that matter, any hearing the risen Christ.[34]

(b) Second, in the third century Origen had already argued for the truth of Christ's resurrection by underlining an observable fact that had to be explained. Despite being proclaimed by uneducated men, the good news of Christ's resurrection spread throughout the world and, against all odds, seemed to be prevailing even at a time when Roman persecution of Christianity was to continue for another century. In Origen's words, 'Jesus' apostles…succeeded in bringing many to obey the word of God by divine power. For in them there was no [human] power of speaking or of giving an ordered narrative by the standards of Greek dialectical or rhetorical arts which convinced their hearers' (*Contra Celsum*, 1.62).[35]

Even more than Origen, Augustine pressed the point and added, as we saw above, that, if 'many noble, eminent, and learned people' had testified to their experience of Christ's resurrection and ascension, it would have been 'perverse to refuse to believe' such witnesses. Granted that the testimony of many such people would have been more weighty than any testimony coming from a few, uneducated persons, nevertheless, the message of the resurrection in any case looked astonishing and questionable, especially as it asked its hearers

---

[32] *Sermons* (184–229Z), trans. Edmund Hill (New Rochelle, NY: New City Press, 1993), 304.

[33] *City of God XI–XXII*, 530.

[34] See G. O'Collins, 'The Appearances of the Risen Christ: A Lexical-exegetical Examination of St Paul and Other Witnesses', *Irish Theological Quarterly* 79 (2014), 128–43, at 136.

[35] Origen, *Contra Celsum*, trans. Henry Chadwick, rev. edn. (Cambridge: Cambridge University Press, 1965), 57.

to change their lives dramatically. Should one agree with Augustine and label as 'perverse' those who might, at least initially, refuse to believe testimony in favour of the resurrection coming from 'many noble, eminent, and learned people'?

(c) Third, Augustine's argument from an observable *effect* (wide acceptance of the faith in Christ's resurrection, despite its being proclaimed by incompetent people from the margins of society) to the only adequate *cause* (the effective truth of that resurrection) should be strengthened. It is not simply that the human resources of the first disciples cannot explain the highly successful propagation of the Easter message. The fate of Jesus himself had created problems that, humanly speaking, were unsurmountable. The public of the day understood his crucifixion as the death of a criminal who, banished from the divine presence, had died cursed by God, and in the place and company of irreligious men (Gal. 3: 13; Heb. 13: 12–13). To honour anyone who had perished in that way was an awful and profound scandal (1 Cor. 1: 23). We cannot explain *either* how the disciples themselves came to believe in such a person as their risen Lord and Saviour *or* how their proclamation of him enjoyed such a striking success, unless Jesus was truly raised from the dead.

Thus Augustine's argument from the observable effects in the history of Christianity to their only adequate and plausible cause (the resurrection) needs to incorporate the shocking and counter-intuitive nature of what they proclaimed. God had raised to glorious, eternal life someone who had died as a criminal rejected by the religious authorities of his time and apparently cursed by God as a blasphemer. What the crucifixion was commonly understood to mean made the message of Christ's resurrection extraordinarily implausible. That God raised to new life someone who had died by crucifixion, by any human reckoning, could not possibly be true. That this message came to be widely accepted was, in Augustine's language, simply 'incredible'.

Now and then in his sermons Augustine introduced the relevant texts from Paul, 1 Corinthians 1: 23 ('Christ crucified, a stumbling block to Jews and foolishness to Gentiles') and Galatians 3: 13 ('Christ became a curse').[36] But he expounded the texts in other ways and

---

[36] On 1 Cor. 1: 23, see s. 150.2 and s. 174.3 (*Sermons* (148–183), trans. Edmund Hill (New Rochelle, NY: New City Press, 1992), 30–1, 259–60); and s. 240.5 (*Sermons* (230–272B), 67–8); see also civ. 10.28 (*City of God XI–XXII*, 338). On Gal.

never pressed them into service to argue that, despite it seeming utterly implausible to Jews and Gentiles, the message about God raising the crucified Jesus had been widely accepted.

(d) Fourth, Augustine's argument from a demonstrable effect to the resurrection being the only adequate cause that can account for this effect has continued in modern times. Some have argued from *the spread of Christianity*, and others from *a novelty to be explained*.

After a short public career, which at most lasted only three or four years, Jesus was abandoned by nearly all his close followers, crucified as a messianic pretender, and apparently rejected by God (Mk. 15: 34), whom he had confidently proclaimed as 'Abba' or 'Father dear'. Yet within a few years the reform movement which he had led within Judaism *spread explosively to become a world religion*. How can we plausibly account for this phenomenon? We can point to certain historical reasons that helped the spread of Christianity: for instance, the coming of the *pax romana*, which enabled relatively easy communication in the first-century Mediterranean world. Add too that slaves, women, and many in the working classes found no other religious option more attractive than Christianity.

Nevertheless, what do matters look like if we follow Hans Küng and compare Jesus with other religious founders?[37] A number of this-worldly factors, which help to explain the propagation of Buddhism, Confucianism, and Islam by the Gautama (d. about 483 BC), Confucius (d. 478 BC), and Muhammad (d. 632 AD), respectively, do not apply to Christianity. In the case of these three founders, time was on their side. Gautama passed most of his long life teaching the way of enlightenment. The Chinese sage Confucius also spent years spreading his wisdom and attracting disciples, until he died and was buried with great pomp outside Kufow. A wealthy wife and then military victories helped Muhammad to gather followers and propagate his teaching and practice. As the recognized prophet of Arabia, he died in Medina and was buried there. In these three very notable cases, we

---

3: 13, see s. 88.8 (*Sermons* (51–94), trans. Edmund Hill (Brooklyn, NY: New City Press, 1991), 424); and s. 377.1 (*Sermons* (341–400), 351).

[37] See H. Küng, *On Being a Christian*, trans. Edward Quinn (London: Collins, 1977), 345.

Arguments for Jesus' Resurrection 47

can point to publicly verifiable causes which furthered the spread, respectively, of Buddhism, Confucianism, and Islam: the long careers of the founders, financial resources, and success in battle. In the case of Christianity, the founder enjoyed none of these advantages: his public career was extremely short; he lacked military and financial support; and his life ended in humiliating failure and a disgraceful death on a cross. After all this, the subsequent propagation of the message of universal salvation in his name remains an enigmatic puzzle, unless we admit a cause (the resurrection) adequate to account for the effect.

Like some others, Küng also appealed to a *religious novelty* that calls out for explanation: the notion of the divine endorsed Messiah being identified as the crucified Jesus.[38] During the ministry of Jesus some of his disciples seem to have accepted him as a messianic agent of divine salvation (e.g. Mk. 8: 29; 11: 1–10). But it is doubtful that they understood and accepted what he said about himself as the suffering Son of Man (e.g. Mk. 8: 31). Then he was executed on the charge of being a messianic pretender and even a blasphemer. What options were available for the disciples after the crucifixion? Could they have modified their messianic belief in him and proclaimed him to be a martyred prophet like John the Baptist and others before him? Hardly, it seems to me. To be crucified was not only to suffer an utterly cruel and humiliating form of execution, but also to die under a religious curse (Gal. 3: 13) and 'outside the camp' of God's covenanted people (Heb. 13: 12–13).[39] In other words, crucifixion was seen as the death of a criminal and godless man who had perished away from God's presence and in the company of irreligious men. To honour anyone who had been put to death in such a way was a profound scandal (1 Cor. 1: 23). Given that crucifixion was such a disgrace, could Jesus' disciples have proclaimed him *even as a martyred prophet*?

In fact, they began preaching the crucified Jesus as the divinely authorized Messiah risen from the dead to bring salvation for all. The

---

[38] Ibid. 371–2.
[39] See Craig R. Koester, *Hebrews* (New York: Doubleday, 2001), 570–1, 576–7.

notion of a Messiah who failed, suffered, was crucified, and then rose from the grave was simply foreign to pre-Christian Judaism. Since their prior religious beliefs could not have led Jesus' disciples to make such startlingly new claims about him, what triggered off this religious novelty. Where did it come from, if not from the resurrection of Jesus himself?

Some modern scholars, when elaborating like Augustine an effect-cause argument, have stressed the centrality of the theme of resurrection in early Christian preaching. Over forty years ago, Christopher Evans showed how 'the central place of the resurrection faith in the New Testament' could not be explained or expected 'either from contemporary Judaism or from the preaching' of Jesus himself.[40] A theme which hitherto had been at best on the religious periphery moved to centre stage. Neither the Jewish background nor the teaching of Jesus sufficiently accounted for the given effect: the central importance which the New Testament attributed to the resurrection. Unless Jesus had been raised from the dead, we have no cause that could adequately explain the centrality of the resurrection in the faith, preaching, and theology of the first Christians.

A similar, more specific form of this effect-cause argument has been mounted by Wolfhart Pannenberg and others about an observable shift in religious expectations. In late Judaism some (in particular, Pharisees) cherished a hope that the resurrection of all the dead and a general judgement would terminate world history. Then the followers of Jesus began proclaiming that one individual had already been raised to a glorious existence which anticipated the end of all history (e.g. 1 Cor. 15: 20–8). What caused such a new element in religious history—the shift from the expectation of general resurrection at the end of history to the proclamation of something that no one had expected, the glorious final resurrection of one individual that had already inaugurated the end? What prompted this radical change in expectations held by one significant group of first-century Jews about the fulfilment of human life through resurrection? Historians of late Judaism have documented the effect, a remarkable change in

---

[40] C. F. Evans, *Resurrection and the New Testament* (London: SCM Press, 1970), 132.

expectations. A plausible cause is available: the actual resurrection of Jesus from the dead.[41]

Once again, just as with arguments about the founding and spread of Christianity, we cannot characterize Pannenberg's argument as a strictly cogent proof. An alternate scenario might be imagined. Some first-century Jews who shared a hope for a general resurrection to come at the end of history could have reflected on the traditions about such individuals as Enoch (Gen. 5: 24) and Elijah (2 Kgs. 2: 9–12) being caught up to heaven and escaping death.[42] This might have triggered an expectation of one or more special individuals being raised from the dead, even before a general resurrection took place. Such a scenario does not, however, strike me as truly plausible. The role ascribed to the risen Jesus for the salvation of the world differs remarkably from any beliefs about Enoch and Elijah.

Where Evans, Pannenberg, Wright, and others have fashioned effect-cause arguments out of demonstrable changes in the beliefs of Jesus' first disciples after his death and burial, Richard Swinburne has named the new celebration of Sunday as the effect to be accounted for.[43] Why did these Jewish disciples no longer give priority to Saturday and turn the first day of the week (e.g. Acts 20: 7; 1 Cor. 16: 2) into *the* day for meeting and worshipping together? What made them hold this day so special that they not only changed their day but also their manner of worship (e.g. 1 Cor. 11: 23–6). An obvious reason is close at hand: Sunday was the day when the tomb of Jesus had been discovered to be open and empty, and the day when they first encountered him raised from the dead.

Without being a strict proof, this argument enjoys a certain plausibility. Those who reject it need to produce an alternate explanation as to

---

[41] W. Pannenberg, *Jesus—God and Man*, trans. L. L. Wilkins and D. A. Priebe (London: SCM Press, 1968), 96. For a much fuller presentation of this argument, see N. T. Wright, *The Resurrection of the Son of God* (London: SPCK, 2003), 372–4, 476–9.

[42] For basic data about the Enoch and Elijah traditions, see J. T. Walsh, 'Elijah', *ABD* ii. 463–6, and R. S. Hess, 'Enoch', *ABD* ii. 508.

[43] R. Swinburne, 'Evidence for the Resurrection', in S. T. Davis, D. Kendall, and G. O'Collins (eds.), *The Resurrection* (Oxford: Oxford University Press, 1997), 191–212; Swinburne included this argument later in *The Resurrection of God Incarnate* (Oxford: Clarendon Press, 2003), 163–70.

why the disciples of Jesus changed their special day of worship—as well as manner of worship—from the Jewish Sabbath to the Christian Sunday.

Two Missing Items Support the Historical Case

We have illustrated how Augustine's effect-cause argument has continued, albeit at times under different forms, right down to the present. But on some questions, Augustine did not take up challenges already faced, for instance, by Origen, challenges that have also been widely and vigorously debated in recent centuries.

As we have seen, Augustine cites eyewitnesses who testified to appearances of the risen Christ. But he does not follow Origen in tackling objections against Mary Magdalene, Peter, and other witnesses—that it was through 'wishful thinking', 'hallucination', or even hysteria that they were deluded into thinking they saw Jesus risen from the dead (*Contra Celsum*, 2.55).[44] In modern times innumerable writers on the resurrection have discussed at length the nature and veracity of the Easter appearances (to individuals and groups) reported in the New Testament. But, unlike Origen, Augustine does not raise these issues, except for what we have noted about his arguing that touching the risen Christ provided the disciples with more certain evidence than merely seeing him.

A second, related 'omission' in Augustine's historical 'apology' for the resurrection concerns the discovery of Jesus' empty tomb. Did Mary Magdalene, alone (Jn. 20: 1–2) or with at least one other female companion (as in the Easter narratives of Mark, Matthew, and Luke), truly find the tomb open and empty on the third day? Modern debates about this question have proved endless. But the question did not concern Augustine. He simply accepted that two men (Joseph of Arimathea and Nicodemus) buried Jesus and that Mary Magdalene, alone or with other women, discovered the tomb to be open and empty. He spoke of the tomb of Jesus when he took up Romans 6: 4 and preached about the baptized sharing sacramentally in Christ's death, burial, and resurrection.[45] Augustine's interest in Jesus' tomb was sacramental, not historical.

---

[44] Origen, *Contra Celsum*, trans. Chadwick, 109.
[45] See s. 229E.3 (*Sermons* (184–229Z), 282).

Miracles and Martyrdom in the Historical Case

Augustine's rhetorical case for the credibility of Christ's resurrection includes an appeal to miracles, both past and present.[46] First, he presses the value of various miracles recorded in the Book of Acts: 'those who had not seen Christ rise in the flesh and ascend with his flesh into heaven believed the men who told of seeing it, because they not only spoke of it but also performed miraculous signs' (civ. 22.5).[47] Augustine recognizes that, to accept this argument, his 'opponents' need to 'concede that these things actually occurred, as we read that they did'. But, 'if they refuse to believe that Christ's apostles really did work these miracles to convince people to believe in their preaching of Christ's resurrection and ascension, they still leave us with one great miracle', which we have seen Augustine develop: 'that the whole world has come to believe it without any miracles at all. And that one miracle is enough for us' (civ. 22.5).[48]

Nevertheless, Augustine shows himself unwilling to drop all appeals to miraculous signs. He is convinced that, in 'the highly educated times' when Christians began preaching the resurrection, miracles did establish the truth of that preaching. People of those days would simply have 'mocked' the idea of 'the resurrection of Christ's flesh and its ascension into heaven' as something 'that could not possibly be true', unless 'the divinity of truth itself, or the truth of divinity, *along with the confirming miraculous signs*, had not shown both that it could take place and that in fact it had taken place' (civ. 22.7; emphasis added).[49] Augustine judges Acts and the rest of the New Testament to be 'supremely truthful books'. Hence he can confidently assert: 'Many miracles have in fact occurred which attest to the one, great, and saving miracle of Christ's ascension into heaven with the flesh in which he rose again' (civ. 22.8).[50]

---

[46] See Petra Schierl, Maria Wittmer-Butsch, and Ephraim Radner, 'Miracles', in Pollmann (ed.), *Oxford Guide to the Historical Reception of Augustine*, iii. 1399–407.

[47] *City of God XI–XXII*, 501. On the historicity of the miracles in Acts, see Joseph A. Fitzmyer, *The Acts of the Apostles* (New York: Doubleday, 1998), 125–6; and Craig S. Keener, *Acts: An Exegetical Commentary*, i (Grand Rapids, MI: Baker Academic, 2012), 320–82.

[48] *City of God XI–XXII*, 501–2.   [49] Ibid. 505.   [50] Ibid. 506.

Second, Augustine reckoned also with the value of miracles in the present. A remarkable passage in *The City of God* (civ. 22.8)[51] reported over twenty recent miracles, which range from someone being cured of gout to people being raised from the dead. Apart from one case that took place when Augustine himself was staying in Milan, all these miracles occurred close to where he lived in North Africa and often in relationship with a shrine of the early martyr, St Stephen. Augustine pressed the apologetic value of the miracles by asking: 'If the resurrection of the flesh to eternal life has not already happened in Christ and if it is not going to happen as Christ himself foretells and as the prophets foretold who foretold Christ, how is it that the dead, who were killed for the very faith that proclaims this resurrection, are able to do such wondrous things?' Augustine answered his own rhetorical question: 'These miracles all bear witness to the faith which proclaims the resurrection of the flesh to eternal life' (civ. 22.9).[52] He accepted and recorded the recent miracles worked through the intercession of martyrs. Having died for their faith in the resurrection of Christ, they could still witness to this faith through the miracles associated with them (civ. 22.9–10).[53]

Yet, all in all, Augustine made more of the witness of martyrdom than he did of miracles. By suffering and dying for the risen Christ and in the hope of sharing his glorious resurrection, martyrs left an inspiring example and testimony to the truth of the resurrection. Here again various predecessors had prepared the way for Augustine. Clement of Rome celebrated the suffering and martyrdom of Peter and Paul (*1 Clement*, 5).[54] Tertullian was at his vivid best in pointing to the powerful witness and fruitful results of those who died for their faith in the risen Christ (*Apologeticum*, 48–50).[55] Origen likewise argued that the sufferings which the Easter witnesses were ready to undergo

---

[51] Ibid. 505–17. Augustine's approach to such miracles is discussed by Peter Brown, *Augustine of Hippo*, rev. edn. (Berkeley, CA: University of California Press, 2000), 416–22.

[52] *City of God XI–XXII*, 518, 519.   [53] Ibid. 518–20.

[54] *Early Christian Writings*, 25–6.

[55] Tertullian, *Apology*, 117–26. In an age when suicide bombers continue to show how they too 'deride the troubles of life', an appeal to martyrdom may have lost some of its force; or at least such an appeal will have to distinguish carefully between self-inflicted death in some allegedly great cause and true martyrdom.

supported the truth of what they proclaimed: '[Jesus] rose again and convinced his disciples about his resurrection, and convinced them to such an extent that they show to all men by their sufferings that they are looking for eternal life and for the resurrection, which has been exemplified before them in word and deed, and [that] they deride all the troubles of life' (*Contra Celsum*, 2.77).[56]

Like his predecessors, Augustine appreciated the powerful witness coming from martyrs, specifically citing St Stephen at whose shrines in North Africa miracles had been taking place. 'To what do all these miracles attest', Augustine asked, 'but the very faith which proclaims that Christ rose in the flesh and ascended into heaven with his flesh? For the martyrs themselves' were 'witnesses to this faith' (civ. 22.9).[57] He respected both the truth that the martyrs proclaimed and the sufferings they endured, but honoured more their 'speaking the truth':

> Let us give our belief, then, to them [the martyrs]. They both *speak the truth* and work wonders. For in *speaking the truth* they suffered, and as a result of their suffering they are able to work wonders. And chief among *the truths they spoke* is *the truth* that Christ rose from the dead and first showed in his own flesh the immortality of the resurrection which he promised would be ours.   (civ. 22.10; emphasis added)[58]

Truth is similarly prominent in the conclusion to a further, powerful passage from Augustine. It draws together the witness of martyrs, the Old Testament prophets' intimations of what was to come, the miraculous 'works of power' that confirmed those intimations, and the efficacious truth of the resurrection which persuaded 'the whole world':

> Despite the terror and oppositions of so many horrible persecutions, the resurrection and immortality of the flesh—first in Christ, then in the rest of us, which will follow in the new age—have been faithfully believed and fearlessly proclaimed. They were sown with the blood of the martyrs to sprout up all the more abundantly throughout the world. For the prior pronouncements of the prophets were read, manifest

---

[56] *Contra Celsum*, 126. St Athanasius had likewise cited the witness of Christians who 'chose to die rather than deny their faith' in the risen Christ (*On the Incarnation*, 27; trans. John Behr (Yonkers, NY: St Vladimir's Seminary Press, 2011), 78).

[57] *City of God XI–XXII*, 518.   [58] Ibid. 520.

works of power confirmed them, and *the truth*—new to custom but not contrary to reason—exercised its persuasive force until the whole world, which once persecuted *the truth* in fury, now followed it in faith. (civ. 22.7; emphasis added)[59]

The closing contrast between persecuting 'the truth in fury' and now following 'it in faith' shows Augustine at his rhetorical best in putting the case for faith in resurrection.

Experience and Desire

Having examined the witness to the truth of Christ's resurrection (and ours) that Augustine drew from 'the outside', namely, from creation and Christian history, we turn now to a further string in his rhetorical bow: the desires and experiences of the human heart on 'the inside'. In a sermon for Easter Monday (preached in 412 or 413 AD), he highlighted something which enabled his audience to believe the preaching of the Easter witnesses: 'You all want to live happy lives. But what is it that makes a person's life happy? What is it that will really make you happy?' He evaluated and rejected various this-worldly stratagems for achieving lasting happiness, and expected that his hearers' experience would prompt them into sharing his conviction: a happy life 'isn't to be found here'. The sermon ended with Augustine putting into the mouth of the risen Christ the following promise:

> I'm inviting you to my life, where nobody dies, where life is truly happy…that's where I'm inviting, to the region of the angels, to the friendship of the Father and the Holy Spirit, to the everlasting supper, to be my brothers and sisters, to be, in a word, myself. I'm inviting you to my life. (s. 231.4, 5)[60]

As a vivid and masterful preacher, Augustine knew how to appeal to the human longing for happiness that can make us ready to accept Christ's resurrection and the promise it communicates.

The human hunger for happiness, with God alone as the final source of happiness, runs like a golden thread through the *City of God*. 'The one

---

[59] Ibid. 505. [60] *Sermons* (230–272B), 21, 22.

God' is the 'giver of happiness' (civ. 4.25),[61] 'the source of our happiness', and 'the end of all desire' (civ. 10.3).[62] Augustine's masterpiece ends with a brilliant evocation of the eternal happiness of the saints who see, love, and praise God (civ. 22.30).[63] As a young man Augustine read *Hortensius*, a dialogue by Cicero which enjoyed a deep and lasting impact on him. (The work is lost and now known mainly through quotations found in Augustine's works.) Cicero's book, Augustine tells us, began 'from an absolutely certain starting point that no one could hesitate about: "We all certainly want to be happy".' Augustine has no doubts about the universal search for happiness: 'that they want to be happy is something all men see in their hearts' (Trin. 13.7, 25).[64] 'Without immortality', Augustine argues, happiness simply 'cannot be', or, as he puts this matter more fully: 'it is altogether impossible for a life to be genuinely happy unless it is immortal'. Through the 'gifts' of the risen and glorified Christ, 'we arrive at the supreme good of immortal happiness' (Trin. 13.10–11, 14).[65]

Centuries later Karl Rahner (1904–84) took a similar line in explaining and justifying Easter faith. The genesis of that faith involves not only the external historical witness coming from Christ's first disciples, but also our inner, transcendental hope, which Augustine had described as our innate desire for blessedness and immortality. For Rahner, a radical orientation towards a total and lasting fulfilment of our existence opens us up to the Easter message, Christ is risen and we will live with him forever.[66] Even more recently, Rowan

---

[61] *The City of God I–X*, 133; see civ. 5, pref. (ibid. 143); civ. 6.12 (ibid. 205); and civ. 8.5 (ibid. 248).

[62] Ibid. 308. The Son of God has 'implanted in us by nature the desire for blessedness and immortality' (civ. 10.29, ibid. 339). See civ. 12.21 (*City of God XI–XXII*, 58–61); civ. 13.17 (ibid. 83); civ. 14.25 (ibid. 133–4); civ. 18.41 (ibid. 323–5); civ. 19.4 (ibid. 354–9); and civ. 19.20 (ibid. 377).

[63] Ibid. 551–4. See John Bussanich, 'Happiness, Eudaemonism', in Fitzgerald (ed.), *Augustine Through the Ages*, 434–7; and P. S. Eardly, 'Happiness', in Pollmann (ed.), *Oxford Guide to the Historical Reception of Augustine*, ii. 1083–7.

[64] *The Trinity*, trans. Edmund Hill (Brooklyn, NY: New City Press, 1991), 348, 364. On the impact that *Hortensius* had on Augustine, see *The Confessions* 3.7–8, trans. Maria Boulding (Hyde Park, NY: New City Press, 1997), 79.

[65] *The Trinity*, 351–2, 354.

[66] K. Rahner, *Foundations of Christian Faith: An Introduction to the Idea of Christianity*, trans. William V. Dych (New York: Crossroad, 1978), 268–78.

Williams wrote of Augustine defining 'the central impulse in human nature' as 'the unqualified desire for God and his truth'.[67]

Such language may put some nerves on red alert, especially for those who recall Ludwig Feuerbach's view that belief in the resurrection is *simply* the projection of our hunger for the happiness of eternal life.[68] Augustine and Rahner would deserve Feuerbach's suspicion if they justified Easter faith merely in terms of a subjective orientation: our hunger for full and lasting happiness (Augustine) or our dynamic, transcendental hope (Rahner). But both Augustine and Rahner recognize the importance of external signs and evidence: the surprising spread of Christianity, accompanied by miracles and the sign of martyrdom (Augustine), and the historical witness of the apostles (Rahner). In their different ways both Augustine and Rahner maintain or at least imply that public evidence converges with personal experience and expectations in creating and sustaining Easter faith.

The Holy Spirit Works in Desire

When we investigate Augustine's rhetorical 'apology' for faith in the resurrection of Christ, we find various elements working together cumulatively. That faith stands in continuity with what he already accepts about God on the basis of creation and its wonders—specifically, the pattern of 'new life after death'. Augustine's 'background theory' about creation and, in particular, the creation of human beings lends credibility to resurrection faith. If nature makes resurrection believable, so too does human history: in particular, the universal spread of Christianity and Christian faith in resurrection, despite the massive difficulty of the first witnesses being a few obscure people of no importance and no education. From a merely human point of view, it was 'incredible' that millions came to believe their testimony to what they had seen, touched, and heard: Christ gloriously risen from the dead. Death by martyrdom attested the truth of their testimony, as did the miracles they worked in their lifetime and the 'modern' miracles that were taking place through their intercession.

---

[67] R. Williams, *On Augustine* (London: Bloomsbury, 2016), 112.

[68] See L. Feuerbach, *The Essence of Christianity*, trans. George Eliot (New York: Harper & Row, 1957), 135–6, 170–84.

Arguments for Jesus' Resurrection

The Easter faith that comes externally 'from hearing' (Rom. 10: 17) the Easter proclamation correlates existentially (our terminology) with the universal search for happiness and answers Augustine's question: 'What will make you really happy?' People 'see in their hearts' this hunger for happiness.

It is in, with, and under this hunger for real and lasting happiness that the Holy Spirit works 'from the inside' as *the* internal witness to produce Easter faith. We quoted Augustine above on 'the divinity of truth' which 'shows' that resurrection can take place 'and has in fact taken place'. 'The divinity of truth' more than hints at 'the Spirit of truth', promised by Jesus at the Last Supper (Jn. 14: 17), a verse that Augustine quotes and associates with John 16: 13 ('when the Spirit of truth comes, he will teach you all truth') (Trin. 1.18)[69]—in first place, the truth of Christ's resurrection, along with all that it implies and promises.

Like John, the apostle Paul also attends to the role of the Holy Spirit, who 'reveals' the 'things of God' (1 Cor. 2: 10–13). Augustine does not neglect this Pauline passage.[70] But other passages seem more relevant: for instance, God 'shines' in the 'heart' of believers so that they know 'the glory of God on the face of [the risen] Christ' (2 Cor. 4: 6).[71] Augustine picks up this verse and associates it with Ephesians 5: 8 when he writes of the resurrection:

> The dawn on which the Lord's resurrection was revealed belongs to the third day; God is suggesting to us by implication that the day now takes its beginning from night—in the sense that he *told light to shine out of darkness* [2 Cor. 4: 6], in order that by the grace of the new covenant and a share in the resurrection of Christ we might hear it said to us, *You were once darkness, but now light in the Lord* [Eph. 5: 8]. (Trin. 4.10)[72]

---

[69] *Trinity*, 77–8. On the Holy Spirit according to Augustine, see Eugene TeSelle, 'Holy Spirit', in Fitzgerald (ed.), *Augustine Through the Ages*, 434–7.

[70] See e.g. civ. 13.24 and 14.4 (*City of God XI–XXII*, 95, 104).

[71] Paul stresses here the inward phenomena or 'shining in human hearts', not the outward, luminous phenomena of the Damascus road encounter that Acts narrates three times (chs. 9, 22, 26); see Murray J. Harris, *The Second Epistle to the Corinthians* (Grand Rapids, MI: Eerdmans, 2005), 333–7.

[72] *Trinity*, 160.

Elsewhere, in a long letter written in 411 or 412 AD, Augustine attributes to the Holy Spirit this 'light' which replaces darkness in the heart. Apropos of Romans 5: 5 (where Paul speaks of 'the love of God poured into our hearts through the Holy Spirit'), Augustine firmly links this love with light. The love infused by the Spirit is also 'the light of the heart' (ep. 140.54).[73]

This light makes possible 'an inner gazing of the heart' (s. 264.2),[74] by which believers see the risen Lord. In a sermon from 396 or 397 AD, Augustine remarked: 'we didn't see him hanging on the cross, nor observe him rising from the tomb. We hold this by faith, we behold it with the eyes of the heart' (s. 263.2).[75]

Augustine clearly understood the resurrection (and ascension) of Jesus Christ to form and fashion the faith and identity of Christians. The extant works of Augustine allow us to put together his case in legitimating such Easter faith. It takes a triple form, appealing to evidence from creation, from Christian history (including miracles and martyrdom), and the inner 'factors' that include the human hunger for happiness. To this third factor, Augustine added the luminous love of the Spirit. This enables believers to behold their risen Lord with 'the eyes of the heart'. Augustine knew the value of a broad, triple-shaped apology for the resurrection. But at the end he recognized that Easter faith is a matter of a Spirit-prompted 'seeing with the heart', a knowing that is loving.

Here Augustine endorsed the deep link between knowing and loving that many other Christian teachers have recognized. Gregory the Great (d. 604) declared: 'love itself is a form of knowing'.[76] In *The Nature and Dignity of Love* William of Saint Thierry (d. 1148) championed the role of love as enlightening reason and making reality intelligible (PL 184, 379–408). His *Exposition of the Song of Songs* circled around the principle '*amor ipse intellectus est*' (love itself is understanding). A few years later Richard of St Victor (d. 1173) expressed this

---

[73] *Letters 100–155*, trans. Roland J. Teske (Hyde Park, NY: New City Press, 2003), 271.

[74] *Sermons* (230–272B), 227.

[75] Ibid. 220; on 'the eyes of the heart', see also doctr. Chr. 4.5.7 (*Teaching Christianity*, 204), and 'the eyes of [your] heart being enlightened' (Eph. 1: 18).

[76] *Homiliae in evangelia*, 27.4 (PL 76, 1207A).

principle by saying, '*ubi amor ibi oculus* (where love exists there is vision)' (*The Book of the Twelve Patriarchs*, ch. 13).[77] In modern times, Bernard Lonergan (d. 1984) famously understood faith to be 'the knowledge born of religious love'.[78]

Conclusion

Over many years Augustine spoke and wrote eloquently and wisely about the resurrection of Jesus Christ. He deployed his rhetorical skills not only to refute philosophical objections to this Easter faith but also, and even more, to encourage the faith of Christians in Jesus' resurrection and all that it promised them.

Augustine recognized how wonder at the constant marvels of created nature, such as the birth of children, predisposes us to believe in the new creation of resurrection. Likewise he contributed to the argument from effects (like the spread against all odds of Christianity) to its only plausible cause (the resurrection of Jesus), which continues vigorously today. He appreciated how the human hunger for full and lasting happiness opens us up, through the internal witness of the Holy Spirit, to become potential hearers of the Easter message. The love and light infused by the Spirit operate in and through the deep connection between knowing and loving. It is 'with the eyes of our heart' that we 'gaze' upon the crucified and risen Jesus.

---

[77] Richard of St Victor, *Selected Writings on Contemplation*, trans. Clare Kirchberger (London: Faber and Faber, 1957), 91. Thomas Aquinas was to use this phrase four times: e.g. in *Super Sent.*, lib. 3. d. 35. q. 1 a. 2. I thank Simon Wayte for this information.

[78] B. F. Lonergan, *Method in Theology* (Toronto: Toronto University Press, 1971), 115.

3
Augustine's Resurrection Faith Updated

The first two chapters of this book have showcased, respectively, Augustine's faith in the resurrection of the crucified Jesus and his rhetorical arguments in support of that faith. His situation long ago as bishop of a small city in North Africa did not mean that he was necessarily worse (or better) placed to understand and interpret the resurrection of Jesus. He was simply differently placed.

If we can truly say of any genuine luminary in the ancient world, 'the dead do not die', this dictum applies eminently to the intellectual and rhetorical giant that Augustine was. The reading public around the globe shows how his words still resonate with modern men and women. Volumes two and three of *The Oxford Guide to the Historical Reception of Augustine* register his impact on a remarkable range of people at the end of the second millennium: from Sophie Scholl (1921–43),[1] guillotined with other members of the White Rose group for opposing Hitler, to the British novelist and scholar, C. S. Lewis (1898–1963).[2]

---

[1] Clive James dedicated to her memory *Cultural Amnesia: Necessary Memories from History and the Arts* (New York: W. W. Norton, 2007), in which he gave her a chapter (pp. 706–14) and said this about her: 'if there can be any such thing as a perfect person beyond Jesus Christ and his immediate family, Sophie Scholl was it' (p. 708).

[2] Karla Pollmann (ed.), *The Oxford Guide to the Historical Reception of Augustine*, iii (Oxford: Oxford University Press, 2013), 1721–2 (Scholl), and 1293–4 (Lewis); see also e.g. C. G. Jung (pp. 1243–6), Jean-Luc Marion (pp. 1367–9), Reinhold Niebuhr (pp. 1448–50), Karl Rahner (pp. 1635–8), Joseph Ratzinger (pp. 1642–5), and Paul Tillich (pp. 1808–10). In volume ii, we find entries evaluating the influence of Augustine on T. S. Eliot (pp. 928–30), Michel Foucault (pp. 1002–4), and Martin Heidegger (pp. 1113–17).

Scholl, Lewis, and many others discovered and organized the teaching of Augustine. In doing so, they updated, corrected, and applied that teaching within their own fields of interest and enquiry. The second half of this book proposes to do something similar for our understanding and interpretation of Jesus' resurrection from the dead.

The three-volume project carried through by Karla Pollmann and her colleagues has encouraged me to attempt a contemporary guide to the creative reception of Augustine's view of Christ's resurrection from the dead. That is the second item in the dual goal of this book. After presenting and assessing what Augustine taught and preached on Jesus' resurrection, my work now aims at bringing Augustine into a modern conversation. Without speaking of creative reception, Rowan Williams brings Augustine into conversation with such modern authors as Hannah Arendt, John Hick, Martha Nussbaum, and Ludwig Wittgenstein.[3]

As a research student at the University of Melbourne, I was introduced to the method of creative reception through a seminar on Plato and Aristotle offered by the late David Armstrong. A close reading of their works preceded a discussion bringing them into conversation with contemporary philosophical issues. Far from looking back at Plato and Aristotle as if their significance were 'merely' historical, Armstrong constantly put the questions: What might we ask them? What might we learn from them? What should we add to their insights? In Armstrong's publications, one can spot places where such questioning bore fruit in his own philosophical thinking.[4]

That said in favour of creative reception, we read Augustine today in the context of the twenty-first century which differs massively from his context in the fourth and fifth century of the Christian era. To be sure, we find clear modern parallels to the perennial questions he raised (for example, is there life beyond death and what will it be like?). But, among many other things, centuries of intellectual achievement and the cultivation of 'scientific' reason may render it challenging to evaluate Augustine's thought and then translate it into current terms.

---

[3] R. Williams, *On Augustine* (London: Bloomsbury, 2016).
[4] See e.g. the references to Plato and Aristotle in D. M. Armstrong, *Belief, Truth, and Knowledge* (Cambridge: Cambridge University Press, 1973), and id., *Truth and Truthmakers* (Cambridge: Cambridge University Press, 2004).

In particular, modern authors, like Richard Swinburne and Karl Rahner (who have already been mentioned in Chapter 2), differ from Augustine (a) philosophically. Others, like Hans Küng and N. T. Wright (also discussed in Chapter 2), differ (b) in the ways they read and interpret the scriptures.

As regards (a), Swinburne brings analytic philosophy to bear on his treatment of Jesus' resurrection. Rahner's philosophy stands in the tradition of Aristotle and Aquinas—not to mention other such influences as Martin Heidegger—as opposed to the Platonic and Neoplatonic philosophy that affected Augustine's thinking. Nevertheless, both the interest Augustine showed in questions of language in *De Doctrina Christiana* and elsewhere and the interest shown by Ludwig Wittgenstein, the *éminence grise* of analytic philosophy, in Augustine's writings should check any desire to see Swinburne and Augustine as philosophically alien to each other. In the case of Rahner, Birgitta Kleinschwärzer-Meister draws attention to certain philosophical (and theological) convergences between Augustine and Rahner that caution against pushing their differences too far.[5]

As regards (b), the development of the historical-critical method and, in general, of modern philosophical hermeneutics takes contemporary scholars away from Augustine when they read and interpret biblical texts.[6] Augustine read the Old Testament scriptures almost exclusively with reference to Christ—an approach to understanding the Hebrew scriptures that calls for serious and nuanced qualifications.[7] He looked in the sacred texts for both a literal and a spiritual (read ecclesiological, moral, and transcendental) meaning. These multiple meanings prepared the way for medieval exegesis to distinguish three different aspects of the spiritual, which related, respectively, 'to

---

[5] See Mark J. Edwards, 'Neoplatonism', in Allan D. Fitzgerald (ed.), *Augustine Through the Ages: An Encyclopedia* (Grand Rapids, MI: Eerdmans, 1999), 588–91; Frederick Van Fleteren, 'Plato, Platonism', ibid. 651–4; B. Kleinschwärzer-Meister, 'Rahner, Karl', in Pollmann (ed.), *Oxford Guide to the Historical Reception of Augustine*, iii. 1635–8; Rudi Te Velde, 'Thomas Aquinas', ibid. 1798–1803; James Wetzel, 'Wittgenstein, Ludwig', ibid. 1914–16.

[6] These changes are well set out in The Pontifical Biblical Commission, *The Interpretation of the Bible in the Church* (Vatican City: Libreria Editrice Vaticana, 1993).

[7] See Pontifical Biblical Commission, *The Hebrew People and their Sacred Scriptures in the Christian Bible* (Vatican City: Libreria Editrice Vaticana, 2001).

the truth revealed, to the way of life commended, and to the final goal to be achieved'.[8]

Augustine's *De Doctrina Christiana* has often been called 'the first Christian essay in hermeneutics'. Yet his approach to biblical interpretation certainly differed from contemporary hermeneutics and, in particular, from that practised in the historical-critical exegesis. Nevertheless, the differences are certainly not total. Moreover, a certain re-evaluation of the limits of the historical-critical method is under way, along with a readiness to accept multiple meanings in biblical texts.[9]

Since philosophical and exegetical differences between Augustine and contemporary scholarship do not pose insuperable differences, a creative reception of his thought seems possible and even worthwhile. Hence this chapter and the next chapter set themselves to the task of retrieving and updating Augustine's teaching and preaching as presented in Chapters 1 and 2, respectively. We will follow the order in which those chapters have treated and assessed what he wanted to say about the resurrection of Christ.

Christ's Resurrection as the Heart of Christian Faith

Augustine, as we saw in Chapter 1, repeatedly highlighted the resurrection of Jesus as the heart of Christian faith and the basis of Christian hope. For Augustine, that faith and hope define Christian identity. From the start of Christianity and so some centuries before the life and ministry of Augustine, the reality of Jesus' resurrection—and sometimes the reality of his death—was denied or radically misinterpreted. Matthew reports how some Jewish opponents alleged that the body of the dead Jesus, despite the setting of a guard, had

---

[8] Biblical Commission, *Interpretation of the Bible*, 78.
[9] See Ludger Schwienhorst-Schönberger, 'Biblical Commentaries, II: From 1700–2000', in Pollmann (ed.), *Oxford Guide to the Historical Reception of Augustine*, ii. 674–8. See also Brenda Deen Schildgen, 'Hermeneutics, I: From Augustine to 1500', ibid. 1126–30; Maarten Wisse, 'Hermeneutics II: From 1500–2000', ibid. 1130–5.

been stolen from the tomb, and that hence there could be no question of his resurrection from the dead (Matt. 28: 15).[10] In the second and third centuries Gnostics claimed that the powers of this lower world failed to harm the heavenly Redeemer and Saviour. They merely succeeded in crucifying a substitute, an image or the fleshly part of Christ, while the spiritual Jesus remained alive and laughed at their mistake.[11]

Recent challenges to Easter faith, or at least to its centrality, can be broadly classified as taking three forms. (a) There are those who simply deny straight out the resurrection of Jesus. Then (b), there are those who twist the meaning of the New Testament's message of Easter, so that it ceases to say anything about the personal fate of Jesus. Finally (c), there are those who admit but marginalize faith in the risen Christ, and do not follow Augustine in what he called believing 'absolutely' in resurrected life (Trin. 2.29).[12] Let us address these forms of resistance and what Augustine might have said in defence of Easter faith and its centrality.

(a) The rise of modern historical consciousness produced by the end of the eighteenth century what Albert Schweitzer called 'the earliest fictitious lives of Jesus', those by Carl Friedrich Bahrdt (1741–92) and Karl Heinrich Venturini (1768–1849), the former's work being 'the sketch' and the latter's 'the finished picture'.[13] According to Bahrdt, the Essenes stage-managed a sham death for Jesus. According to Venturini, by accident or good fortune, Jesus was taken down from the cross unconscious but still alive; with the help of the Essene brethren, he revived, lived on, and took leave of his disciples in a scene that they mistakenly interpreted as his ascension into heaven.

---

[10] On the story of the setting and bribery of the guard, see Ulrich Luz, *Matthew 21–28*, trans. J. E. Crouch (Minneapolis: Fortress, 2005), 585–9, 609–13; John Nolland, *The Gospel of Matthew* (Grand Rapids, MI: Eerdmans, 2005), 1234–9, 1254–8; and N. T. Wright, *The Resurrection of the Son of God* (London: SPCK, 2003), 636–40.

[11] See Pheme Perkins, *The Gnostic Dialogue: The Early Church and the Crisis of Gnosticism* (New York/Ramsey: Paulist Press, 1980), 114, 118, 121, 146, 180, 186.

[12] *The Trinity*, trans. Edmund Hill (Brooklyn, NY: New City Press, 1991), 118.

[13] A. Schweitzer, *The Quest of the Historical Jesus*, trans. W. Montgomery (New York: Macmillan, 1961; German orig. 1906), 38–47, at 44.

Schweitzer reported others like H. E. G. Paulus and F. E. D. Schleiermacher who portrayed Jesus as recovering from a death-like trance after being removed from the cross. At the end of a section on Venturini, Schweitzer remarked that his life of Jesus 'may almost be said to be reissued annually down to the present day, for all the fictitious "lives" go back to the style which he [Venturini] created. It is plagiarized more freely than any other life of Jesus, although practically unknown by name.'[14]

In a co-authored article, Daniel Kendall and I examined works by (in this order) George Moore, D. H. Lawrence, Robert Graves, Hugh Schonfield, John Updike, Donovan Joyce, Michael Baigent, Richard Leigh, Henry Lincoln, Duncan Derrett, Soami Divyanand, and Barbara Thiering. We showed how Schweitzer's claim about 'plagiarism' was broadly justified.[15] In a review of Derrett's thesis about Jesus surviving crucifixion, T. S. M. Williams declared it to be simply 'unbelievable', and made a criticism that touches all these authors: 'that Christianity is the outcome of a freak turn of events' rather than 'the fruit of his [Jesus'] whole life sealed by his death on the cross [and his resurrection] is hard to swallow'.[16]

Most scholars, but not Schweitzer and the editors of the *Journal of Theological Studies*, have been inclined to dismiss all these modern, Venturini-inspired works as mere curiosities and pseudo-scholarship. But sometimes they become mega-sellers that the media and the wider public take seriously. If he were alive today, Augustine would, I believe, have been prompted by his pastoral responsibility and love of truth to attend to such books, which, as a matter of fact, challenge and harm the Easter faith of many people. Let me take one contemporary case to exemplify what I have in mind.

To much fanfare and in time for Easter 2010, Philip Pullman published *The Good Man Jesus and the Scoundrel Christ*,[17] a historical

---

[14] Ibid. 471; see 326–9; on Paulus see ibid. 53–5; on Schleiermacher, see ibid. 64–5.

[15] G. O'Collins and D. Kendall, 'On Reissuing Venturini', *Gregorianum* 75 (1994), 241–65.

[16] *Journal of Theological Studies* 36 (1985), 445–7.

[17] Edinburgh: Canongate, 2010. See G. O'Collins, *Philip Pullman's Jesus* (London: Darton, Longman, and Todd, 2010).

novel in which he retold the story of Jesus by inventing 'the fable' of a twin for the historical Jesus. He mixed the fable (which, by definition, is not based on history) with fact, the undoubted historical existence of Jesus. The normally accepted requirements for historical fiction raised a further issue. Did Pullman think there could be any plausibility whatsoever in making 'Christ', as he did, the one and only source on which all four Gospels drew to tell their story of Jesus? This fictional twin, influenced by a sinister 'stranger', falsified the record of Jesus' ministry, betrayed his brother to death, and then masqueraded as Jesus risen from the dead. Let us see in detail Pullman's reconstruction of the death of Jesus and its aftermath. Augustine would have waxed eloquent about its blatant implausibility and disregard for something Augustine treasured deeply, truth in all its forms.[18]

Pullman's retelling of the Gospel stories respects the role of Pilate's ruthless brutality in despatching Jesus to his death on the cross. He plays down the responsibility of Caiaphas and represents him as suggesting that Pilate send Jesus into exile. What Caiaphas says about the expediency of Jesus' death (Jn. 11: 49) is maintained but conveniently put into the mouths of the 'stranger' and Christ, the twin brother of Jesus who plays the part of Judas.[19] Christ is paid to lead the guard to Jesus and identify him with a kiss. In Pullman's version he does not, however, then give way to remorse, return the money to the chief priests, and hang himself (Matt. 27: 3–10). Instead, in Pullman's rewriting of the story, Christ (alias 'Judas') agrees to do something worse by pretending to be his dead brother and so deceive people into thinking that Jesus had risen from the dead.

The 'stranger' has convinced Christ that the 'truth' (read lie) of the resurrection is necessary. This lie will bring great comfort to the sick, the starving orphans, and to dying women. The page where the 'stranger' puts the case for fabricating Jesus' resurrection is, in my view, the most cynical in the whole book.[20]

---

[18] See Simon Harrison, 'Truth, Truths', in Fitzgerald (ed.), *Augustine through the Ages*, 852–3; and Robert Kennedy, 'Falsehood', in Pollmann (ed.), *The Oxford Guide to the Historical Reception of Augustine*, ii. 975–9.

[19] Pullman, *The Good Man Jesus*, 174.   [20] Ibid.

As in the Gospel narratives, Joseph of Arimathea, assisted by Nicodemus, sees to the honourable burial of Jesus. The 'stranger' organizes several men to remove the body of Jesus during the night of Saturday/Sunday. He persuades Christ to return the following morning and play the part of the 'risen' Jesus. Mary Magdalene, who has discovered the tomb to be open and empty, then meets and talks with the twin brother of Jesus. She thinks she has seen the risen Jesus and runs to announce the wonderful news to the other disciples.

Later the same day, the disciples, including Thomas, set off as a group for a village called Emmaus. Christ joins them on the road. They reach the village at night and invite him to join them for a meal. A disciple called Cleopas brings a lamp close to Christ's face and takes him to be the risen Jesus. Christ plays out the deception, encourages the disciples to identify him as his twin brother raised from the dead, and, for good measure, leaves them with a 'sign' of his brother's resurrection from the dead: bread that is to be broken and wine that is to be poured out.

Many of those who reviewed Pullman's retelling of the Jesus story found little plausibility in the way he 'explains' away the empty tomb and the Easter appearances.[21] The only 'new' item added by Pullman to such earlier 'explanations' comes when he attributes the removal of Jesus' corpse to a villainous 'stranger' who is intent on creating organized Christianity.

If he were commenting today on Pullman's book, Augustine would doubtless have pointed out how he ignores the appearances of the risen Jesus in Galilee (Matt. 28: 16–20; Jn. 21; and implied by Mk. 16: 7); the appearance to Peter (1 Cor. 15: 5; Lk. 24: 34); the appearance to 'more than five hundred' disciples (1 Cor. 15: 6); the appearance to Paul (1 Cor. 9: 1; 15: 8; Gal. 1: 12, 15–16; Acts 9; 22; 26). Pullman selects the appearance to Mary Magdalene (Jn. 20: 11–19) and the Emmaus story (Lk. 24: 13–35), into which he slots the appearance to Thomas (Jn. 20: 24–9).

Some reviewers have spotted a hint of chauvinism in the way Pullman represents the credulity of Mary Magdalene. She meets the

---

[21] For a list of these reviews (and interviews), see O'Collins, *Philip Pullman's Jesus*, 101–2.

68   *Saint Augustine on the Resurrection of Christ*

twin of Jesus and imagines that she has seen Jesus himself risen from the dead. This kind of way of 'explaining' Mary's experience at the tomb has a long history. It reaches back through the *Life of Jesus* by Ernest Renan (d. 1892) to Celsus in the second century. Renan built up Mary as *the* (hallucinated) witness, whose passionate love made her imagine that Jesus was personally risen from the dead and whose testimony convinced the other disciples.[22] In his *True Discourse*, the earliest book that we know to have been written against Christianity, Celsus dismissed Mary as a 'hysterical female', who, seemingly together with Peter, created belief in the resurrection of Jesus (quoted by Origen in *Contra Celsum*, 2.55).[23] Augustine did not know this work by Origen, and so could not take up what Origen reported about Celsus explaining away the post-resurrection experience of Mary Magdalene.[24]

As regards the Emmaus story, Pullman feels free to play games with what he reads in Luke, where only two disciples walk to the village and then recognize Jesus in the 'breaking of the bread'. Pullman rewrites, rather than re-tells, a vivid and beloved Easter story, for which the brilliance of Luke's writing has been matched by masterpieces coming from Caravaggio, Rembrandt, and other classical artists.

I can understand the reaction of A. N. Wilson[25] to Pullman's caricature of the Easter stories. Pullman not only remains silent about so much testimony to post-resurrection appearances of Jesus but also leaves us with a strange puzzle. In tones that recall Augustine (see Chapter 2), Wilson asks: could the early Christian witnesses have lived such heroic lives and spread the message of Jesus with such devotion, if all that lay behind their missionary outreach were fraud

---

[22] Renan wrote: 'The strong imagination of Mary Magdalene played an important part in the matter [establishing belief in Christ's resurrection]. Divine power of love! Sacred moments in which the passion of one possessed gave the world a resuscitated God' (Ernest Renan, *The Life of Jesus*, trans. William G. Hutchison (London: Walter Scott, 1898), 272).

[23] Origen, *Contra Celsum*, trans. Henry Chadwick, rev. edn. (Cambridge: Cambridge University Press, 1965), 109.

[24] From the 390s, Augustine came to know firsthand some works by Origen, but, apparently, not *Contra Celsum*; see Joseph W. Trigg, 'Origen', in Fitzgerald (ed.), *Augustine Through the Ages*, 603–5.

[25] *The Spectator*, 3 April 2010.

Augustine's Resurrection Faith Updated 69

(namely, the theft of Jesus' body), and two episodes in which first a credulous woman (Mary Magdalene) and then a group (the disciples at Emmaus) mistook the identity of someone they met—a mistaken identification, deliberately prompted by a twin of Jesus masquerading as his dead brother brought back to life? That such a fraudulent turn of events after the burial of Jesus was sufficient to cause the rise and spread of Christianity will convince only the credulous, or rather those who cannot imagine that there is a God who raised Jesus from the dead and gave him a new and glorious life. They would rather entertain far-fetched 'explanations' than accept the resurrection of Jesus as it truly happened.

Pullman's version of what happened after the death of Jesus is so contrived and plays so fast and loose with the historical evidence that it loses even superficial plausibility. At the end, does Pullman turn the greatest story ever told into the greatest puzzle ever imagined? To be sure, he is writing historical fiction. But, by its very nature, *historical* fiction should be plausible—also from a historical point of view. Augustine, I think, would have firmly countered Pullman on the grounds of historical plausibility.

Pullman's book vindicates what Augustine preached about the resurrection of Jesus being 'the distinctive mark of the Christian faith'. Hence, Augustine concluded, 'this is what defines our faith, the resurrection of the Lord Jesus Christ' (s. 229H1, 3).[26] As we might put it today, Christianity stands or falls with the resurrection. Pullman has taken aim at the very heart of Christianity by suggesting that it was founded on deliberate fraud, not on a true resurrection of Jesus, but on the theft of his body, and encounters with his twin pretending to be Jesus risen from the dead. Without explicitly saying as much, Pullman agrees with Augustine by implying that Jesus' rising from the dead defines the faith of Christians and establishes their identity. In making his attack on the resurrection, Pullman knows how high the stakes are.

(b) Augustine would have deployed his unrelenting intelligence also against those who, in various ways, have developed the thesis that

[26] *Sermons* (184–229Z), trans. Edmund Hill (New Rochelle, NY: New City Press, 1993), 295, 297.

what happened after the death and resurrection of Jesus was *merely* a change in the hearts and minds of his disciples, not a new, transformed life for Jesus himself. Thus, for Geza Vermes, Jesus 'rose' only in the sense of now being followed and loved by his disciples.[27]

As such this thesis was not around in Augustine's day and could not be refuted by him. He exhibited, nevertheless, a robust sense that the resurrection was, first and above all, a new event affecting Jesus himself. Right from Chapter 1, we noted how Augustine repeatedly quoted Romans 10: 9: 'if you confess with your lips that Jesus is Lord and believe in your heart that God raised him from the dead, you will be saved' (quoted en. Ps. 120.7).[28] The basic problem with any 'mere change of heart thesis' is that it must deny the obvious meaning of what Paul and other New Testament authors repeatedly say, and say in a variety of ways.

Let me take one example: the formula of proclamation cited by Paul: 'I handed on to you…what I in turn had received that Christ *died* for our sins in accordance with the scriptures, and that he *was buried* and that he *was raised*…and that he *appeared* to Cephas [Peter], then to the twelve' (1 Cor. 15: 3–5; emphasis added). In this formula, Christ is the subject of all four verbs, the last two ('was raised' and 'appeared') just as informative as the first two ('died' and 'was buried'). In the case of both pairs of verbs, the second verb explains and supports what the first claims. We know that Christ died because he was buried; burial points to a prior death. We know that Christ has been raised because he appeared bodily alive to a number of individuals and groups; dead persons do not appear like that.

For all the sincerity with which Vermes and others have put forward their thesis, they must suppose that Paul and other New Testament writers, although seeming to claim some new fact about Jesus (his personal resurrection from death to new life), were using a deceptive form of discourse and *merely* talking about a fresh love that possessed their hearts. They spoke only of themselves, not of a new event affecting Jesus himself.

---

[27] See G. Vermes, *The Resurrection* (New York: Doubleday, 2008), 149–52.
[28] *Expositions of the Psalms* (99–120), trans. Maria Boulding (Hyde Park, NY: New City Press, 2003), 67.

Augustine's Resurrection Faith Updated 71

Are we to imagine that the New Testament authors were deliberately deceptive in their use of language? Or were they remarkably incompetent? These are the only plausible alternatives open to us if we allege that their assertions about Jesus' resurrection were *merely* assertions about themselves. Vermes and others who feel free to redefine the original Easter message are, in effect, claiming to know better than the New Testament authors what those authors meant when they wrote what they did.[29]

(c) Finally, Augustine would not be happy with what has happened (or rather what has not happened) in various theological disciplines developed long after his time. Experts in some branches of Christian theology, without rejecting the resurrection of Christ, can strangely neglect it in the course of teaching their specific disciplines. This has proved the case, for instance, in the areas of sacramental and moral theology (perhaps better called 'Christian ethics'). Teachers and authors in these two fields have often failed to reflect on the resurrection and let it 'saturate' their thinking. Yet Christ's resurrection provides the broadest horizon within which we can recognize what the sacraments mean and how we should live.

There have been happy exceptions: such as German Martinez, who incorporates the resurrection into a pastoral presentation of the seven sacraments.[30] But he largely remains an exception in sacramental theology. In 1997 Brian Johnstone published a seminal article on the place of the resurrection in the area of moral theology. But nothing much seems to have changed. Christian reflection on the moral life has continued to be largely unaffected by the event of Jesus' resurrection and the hope it embodies. Augustine would find the continuing neglect of the resurrection in Christian ethics and sacramental theology very strange. Johnstone's article also highlighted the way in which a resurrection-oriented morality will go hand in hand with a Trinity-oriented morality. But contemporary Christian

---

[29] For further material on such attempts to re-interpret the essential Easter claim about the risen Jesus, see G. O'Collins, *Believing in the Resurrection* (Mahwah, NJ: Paulist Press, 2012), 50–5.

[30] G. Martinez, *Signs of Freedom: Theology of the Christian Sacraments* (Mahwah, NJ: Paulist Press, 2003).

ethics also reveal an extraordinary silence about the Trinity, the identity of God disclosed in the events of Easter and Pentecost.[31]

To sum up. Over against 'Jews and pagans', Augustine proclaimed the truth of Jesus' resurrection and its absolute centrality for Christian faith. Through Matthew's Gospel, he knew, of course, of an early attempt to discredit the resurrection by alleging that the disciples stole the body by night when the guard were asleep. Naturally Augustine, followed by Thomas Aquinas, ridiculed the idea of the guards being in a position to testify to something that supposedly happened when they were sleeping.[32] For all its sophistication, Pullman's book proposes a latter-day version of 'the-body-being-stolen-by-night' thesis. If Augustine did happen to know of some Gnostic theory which denied the resurrection by asserting that a substitute of Jesus, but not Jesus himself, was crucified, he did not think it worthy of attention.

Augustine lived, of course, centuries before (a) Venturini put into circulation the 'swoon' theory: the execution of Jesus was bungled and he survived to live on with the Essene community or somewhere else. Nor did Augustine know in advance about (b) the 'new consciousness' thesis of some modern writers, according to which the New Testament claims that Jesus 'rose' but merely in the sense of the minds and hearts of his disciples being changed. (c) Augustine lived long before Christian theology, developed into its various branches, has sometimes or even often—for instance, in the areas of sacramental and moral theology—drawn little or nothing from Easter faith. With his unqualified acceptance of the resurrection of Jesus and its central importance, Augustine would have taken issue with those who can be gathered under (c), as well as those who fit under (a) and (b).

---

[31] See O'Collins, *Believing in the Resurrection*, 170–1; for details on the neglect of the resurrection in sacramental and moral theology, see ibid. 154–71, 210–13.

[32] As Ulrich Luz reports Augustine and Aquinas, 'if the guards had been awake, they would have had to chase the disciples away. If they were asleep, they could not have seen it [the disciples approaching to steal the body]. Thus it is obvious that it [their story] was a lie' (*Matthew 21–28*, trans. James E. Crouch (Minneapolis: Fortress Press, 2005), 611, n. 15).

Christ Raised or Risen from the Dead

We noted in Chapter 1 how Augustine characteristically followed later New Testament usage by presenting Jesus as rising through his own power. He took up the Johannine language about Jesus' own divine power effecting his personal resurrection. Yet he knew Romans very well and often quoted Paul's words in Romans 8: 9: 'God raised him [Jesus] from the dead'. Augustine also cited what Romans says about the Holy Spirit in 8: 10–11: 'if the Spirit of God who *raised Jesus from the dead* dwells in you, he who *raised Jesus from the dead* will give life to our mortal bodies through the Holy Spirit who dwells in you' (s. 362.24; emphasis added).[33] Nevertheless, instead of following Paul in representing Jesus' resurrection as God (the Father) acting through the Holy Spirit, Augustine left the apostle behind and expressly took up John's way of picturing Christ as bringing about the resurrection through his own divine power.

This move meant that Augustine missed the chance of adopting fully the Trinitarian theology of Paul, or the apostle's speaking of the Father, Son, and Holy Spirit in relational or mutually defining terms. As Wesley Hill has argued, in the theology of Paul, the identities of God, Jesus, and the Spirit are to be primarily construed by their relations with one another.[34] Thus to identify Jesus we must refer to God, with whom Jesus is the co-bearer of the divine name, *Kyrios* (e.g. Phil. 2: 11). In turn God is identified by actions done by, to, and in Jesus, who is 'sent' (Gal. 4: 4), 'died for the ungodly' (Rom. 5: 6), and 'was exalted' (Phil. 2: 9). In particular, Paul repeatedly identifies God (the Father) as the One who has raised Jesus from the dead (e.g. Rom. 4: 24; 2 Cor. 4: 14; Gal. 1: 1; 1 Thess. 1: 10). The fatherhood of God and the sonship of Jesus are constituted in and through the Holy Spirit, who raised Jesus from the dead and raises the dead. Jesus is the Son of God in power by the action of the Spirit of holiness, who is the means by whom God raises the dead (Rom. 1: 3–4; 8: 9–11). In this way the resurrection of Jesus prompts Paul into understanding the

---

[33] *Sermons* (341–400), trans. Edmund Hill (Hyde Park, NY: New City Press, 1995), 260.

[34] W. Hill, *Paul and the Trinity: Persons, Relations, and the Pauline Letters* (Grand Rapids, MI: Eerdmans, 2015).

Trinitarian relations between God (the Father), Jesus (the Son), and the Holy Spirit—an insight into the apostle's teaching on the resurrection not shared by Augustine.

However, Augustine does pick up the Trinitarian implications to be detected when Paul characterizes the Spirit as both 'the Spirit of God' (e.g. 1 Cor. 12: 3) and 'the Spirit of Jesus/Christ the Son' (e.g. Gal. 4: 6)—that is to say, as inseparable from, and simultaneously distinct from, the Father and the Son. Augustine writes of the way 'holy' and 'spirit' can be predicated of the Trinity as a whole: 'because Father and Son and Holy Spirit are one God, and because God of course is holy and *God is spirit* [Jn. 4: 24], the triad can be called both holy and spirit'. Yet Augustine draws from Paul a way of referring the divine persons to each other: 'insofar as he [the Holy Spirit] is properly or peculiarly called the Holy Spirit, [and] is so called relationship-wise [through] being referred to both Father and Son... the Holy Spirit is the Spirit of the Father and of the Son' (Trin. 5.12).[35] Augustine recognizes that these relationships of which Paul writes are asymmetrical. It would be misleading to speak either of 'God the Father of the Spirit' or of 'Christ the Son of the Spirit' (Trin. 5.13).[36] The Trinitarian relationships indicated by Paul, while mutual, are irreversible. Full interdependence of Father, Son, and Spirit does not entail their being interchangeable.

Thus Augustine's teaching on the resurrection of Jesus might have been further enriched by drawing on a typically Trinitarian way in which Paul presents it. Augustine hints at a Trinitarian understanding of the resurrection found in the apostle's letters. But he could have drawn more from Paul's letters to fill out this specific understanding of the Easter mystery.

---

[35] *Trinity*, 197.

[36] Ibid. 198. Later in *The Trinity*, Augustine moves the event of the resurrection away from what we find implied by Paul's language of the Spirit being 'the Spirit of the Father' and 'the Spirit of the Son': 'according to the holy scriptures [read Paul and John] the Holy Spirit is not just the Father's alone nor the Son's alone, but the Spirit of them both, and thus he suggests to us the common charity with which the Father and the Son love each other' (Trin. 15.27; ibid. 418; see 15.37; ibid. 424).

The New Life of the Risen Christ

Chapter 1 of this book cited passages from Augustine where he described the risen existence of Christ as 'immortal', 'incorruptible', and 'spiritual'. Augustine summarized this development by speaking of Christ undergoing not a loss of his body but a 'change in its quality', which also included a new 'brightness', even if this brightness was hidden from the eyes of Peter, Mary Magdalene, and the other disciples when they met him after his resurrection from the dead. Yet, rather than dwelling on new qualities of Christ's post-resurrection bodily existence, Augustine often attended to its 'sameness', which enabled the disciples to recognize him by 'seeing' him, but, even more, by 'touching' him. Christ rose with/in 'the very same body', which they touched.

What counts here as 'the very same' or, as we might put it, 'the identical' body? We saw how Augustine, to avoid an over-spiritualized view of the resurrection, argued that after the resurrection 'the flesh of our Lord Jesus Christ' maintained 'human functions'. This was to convince the disciples that 'what had been buried' had 'also risen again'. The specific function that Augustine had in mind was eating and drinking. The risen Christ 'ate and drank', not because 'he was thirsty and hungry' or that there was some need 'to restore tissues', but to 'persuade his disciples of the true reality of his body' (s. 362.10, 12).[37] Augustine denied that the risen Jesus could suffer any loss of 'strength and energy' that needed to be 'recharged' by eating and drinking[38] He ate and drank only to convince others that he had risen in the true flesh of the same body which had been buried in the tomb.

Here one should challenge Augustine's interpretation on the exegetical front: first, about (a) his preference for touching over seeing when reporting what the New Testament says about the post-resurrection encounters, and (b) his interpretation of the fish-eating episode in Luke 24. Was it more important that Jesus in his bodily, resurrected condition was tangible rather than visible? Did his risen existence allow him to eat (and drink), albeit not out of necessity (as during his earthly existence)?

---

[37] *Sermons* (341–400), 247, 249–50.   [38] Ibid. 248.

(a) First, the New Testament reports only two cases of people touching Christ in the post-resurrection encounters: two women (Mary Magdalene and 'the other Mary') 'took hold of his feet and worshipped him' (Matt. 28: 9), and one woman (Mary Magdalene) 'clung' to the risen Jesus when he disclosed himself to her (Jn. 20: 17). In both cases the point at issue is the appropriate, new way of relating to the risen Christ rather than the state of the risen body and the possibility of touching it. In Matthew's brief account, the two women, by worshipping Jesus, already embrace this new way of relating to Christ. In John's version, Mary Magdalene has to learn to relate to Christ in this new way.

In Luke 24: 19, the risen Jesus invites the frightened and bewildered disciples: '*look* at my hands and my feet; *see* that it is I myself. Touch me and *see*, for a ghost does not have flesh and bones, as you *see* that I have.' In John 20: 27, Jesus addresses in similar terms only Thomas: 'Put your finger here and *see* my hands. Reach out your hand and put it in my side' (emphasis added). But, *pace* later commentators and painters, we are *not* told that either the disciples or Thomas took up the invitation and literally touched Jesus.[39] Thomas, in fact, at once blurted out his confession, 'my Lord and my God', and elicited from Jesus the response: 'have you believed because you have seen [*not touched*] me?' (Jn. 20: 28–9). He did not verify what he had seen by touching the risen body of Christ. In both Luke and John, the invitation to touch the risen Jesus is more than balanced by a repeated use of 'see', not to mention 'look' in Luke 24: 39. A certain rhetorical exaggeration affected what Augustine said in a sermon probably preached in 411 AD: 'they [the disciples] felt and handled the solidity of his body, since it wasn't enough for some of them to see what they remembered, unless they could also touch what they saw' (s. 361.8).[40]

---

[39] Apropos of Christ showing his hands and his side in Jn. 20: 20, Andrew T. Lincoln writes: 'Rather than demonstrating that Jesus was not some form of ghost, as in Luke 24: 37, or serving as an anti-docetic polemic, this display simply underscores the identity of the risen Lord with the crucified Jesus, whose hands had been nailed to the cross and…side pierced with a spear' (*The Gospel According to John* (London: Continuum, 2005), 497). Thomas 'comes to faith not because he actually touches Jesus' hands and side—there is no indication that he takes up Jesus' invitation' (ibid. 503).

[40] *Sermons* (341–400), 230.

Augustine's Resurrection Faith Updated

For the sake of completeness (and not because Augustine brings up this case), we should mention what, in the Book of Revelation, John says when recounting the vision of the glorious Christ that he experienced on the Lord's day: 'when I saw him, I fell at his feet as though dead. But he placed his right hand on me, saying: "Do not be afraid, I am the first and the last, the Living One…Now write what you have seen, what is, and what is to take place after this"' (Rev. 1: 17–19). This apocalyptic vision, far from being one of the post-resurrection encounters to which the visionary testifies and which could shed some light on the nature of the risen body, serves rather to introduce the book that follows and establish the authority vested in the author.[41]

Over against Augustine's highlighting and, to an extent, misinterpreting the few verses that might involve touching the risen Lord, the New Testament shows a different emphasis. When it comes to the first disciples experiencing the risen Christ, the language of sight predominates. The disciples' decisive experience of the Easter Jesus involved seeing him.

A form of the common verb 'to see (*horaō*)', *ōphthē* (he appeared, he became visible, he let himself be seen) featured prominently in references to the post-resurrection encounters with the risen Jesus (e.g. Lk. 24: 34; Acts 13: 31; 1 Cor. 15: 5, 6, 7, 8). The New Testament employs *ōphthē* to identify visionary or visible appearances of the risen Christ, or what we might call 'Christophanies'. Ananias uses the related participle *ophtheis* to speak of 'Jesus who appeared to you [Paul] on the road' (Acts 9: 17). The risen Christ himself says to Paul: 'I have appeared (*ōphthēn*) to you, for this purpose, to appoint you to serve and to testify to the things which you have seen in me, and to those in which I will appear (*ophthēsomai*)' (Acts 26: 16).

Add too the use of *ōphthē* in a hymnic or, more likely, a creedal fragment in 1 Timothy: 'He [Christ Jesus] appeared to messengers' (1 Tim. 3: 16). Normally '*aggelois*' has been translated here as 'angels', creating a question: how could the risen Christ appear to beings of

---

[41] Craig Koester writes: 'Traditionally, a person overcome by a heavenly presence was given a word of assurance (Tob. 12: 17), sometimes with the touch of a hand (Dan. 10: 10, 12)…The powerful right hand that holds the seven stars is also used to give John assurance (Rev. 1: 16, 20)' (*Revelation: A New Translation with Introduction and Commentary* (New Haven: Yale University Press, 2014), 247).

another world, angels? But in the New Testament '*aggeloi*' can also designate human messengers: for instance, John the Baptist (Matt. 11: 10; Mk. 1: 2; Lk. 7: 27), messengers sent by the Baptist (Lk. 7: 24), and Paul himself (Gal. 4: 14). Hence some major commentaries translate the passage from 1 Timothy as 'he appeared to messengers', understanding these to be the witnesses who went on to proclaim the resurrection of Jesus. The phrase puts together the three individuals and three groups that Paul lists in 1 Corinthians 15: 5–8.[42]

Closely linked to the Christophany language are the many references to 'seeing' the risen Christ: for instance, 'he [the resurrected Christ] is going before you into Galilee; there you will see (*opsesthē*). him' (Mk. 16: 7; see Matt. 28: 7, 10). 'Seeing' him on the mountain, the eleven disciples adore him (Matt. 28: 17). Mary Magdalene joyfully announces, 'I have seen (*heōraka*) the Lord' (Jn. 20: 18). Barnabas explains that Saul 'saw (*eiden*) the Lord on the road' (Acts 9: 27). Thomas comes to faith because he has 'seen' the risen Christ; those are blessed who come to faith without have seen the risen Christ, as the original witnesses did (Jn. 20: 29; see 1 Pet. 1: 8). Likewise Paul (in 1 Cor. 9: 1) implies that the Corinthians have not experienced what he has experienced—his 'seeing' (the risen Lord) should be distinguished from any later coming to Christian faith on the part of those who are not the original, apostolic witnesses.

Besides the verb *horaō*, when reporting Easter appearances, Luke 24: 37 and 39 and John 20: 12, 14 use in the active another verb 'to see', '*theōrein*'. John also employs the active voice of '*phaneroun*', 'to show' (Jn. 21: 1 twice) and once the passive '*ephanerōthē*' (Jn. 21: 14). At the end of the story about the two disciples at Emmaus, 'their eyes were opened and they recognized him [the risen Christ] and he vanished (*aphantos egeneto*) from their sight' (Lk. 24: 31). In speaking of

---

[42] Luke Timothy Johnson, *The First and Second Letters to Timothy* (New York: Doubleday, 2001), 233; Jerome D. Quinn and William C. Wacker, *The First and Second Letters to Timothy* (Grand Rapids, MI: Eerdmans, 2000), 297, 337–48. Philip H. Towner, *The Letters to Timothy and Titus* (Grand Rapids, MI: Eerdmans, 2006), 281–2, considers a reference to human 'messengers' possible but prefers to translate 'angels'. I. Howard Marshall, *The Pastoral Epistles* (London: T. & T. Clark, 1999), 526–7, likewise notes the possibility of human messengers, but renders '*aggeloi*' as 'angels'.

the appearance of the risen Jesus to Mary Magdalene, to the two disciples, and to the eleven, the longer ending of Mark's Gospel employs the passive voice of '*theaomai*' (Mk. 16: 11) and of '*phaneroun*' (Mk. 16: 12, 14) and the middle voice of '*phainō*' (Mk. 16: 9). Acts speaks of the risen Christ 'presenting himself alive' and 'appearing (*optanomenos*)' (Acts 1: 3) and 'being allowed to appear (*emphanē genesthai*)' (Acts 10: 4).

Enough data should have been now produced to establish how the appearance narratives in the Gospels and Acts converge with Paul (and 1 Timothy). In their choice of verbs, they all witnessed the Easter encounters as being somehow ocular and visual. In some narratives—classically in the Emmaus story of Luke 24—disciples fail to recognize immediately the risen Lord. But such delayed recognition does not negate the ways in which Paul, the Gospels, and Acts heavily apply the language of sight to the meetings with the risen Jesus. Augustine's stress on touching fails to match the New Testament witness, for which 'seeing' the risen Lord easily predominates over 'touching' him. It is clearly much more important for the New Testament Christians that the body of the risen Lord was visible and much less important that he was tangible. In Chapter 4 we will have occasion to reflect further on what seeing the risen Christ involved.[43]

(b) Second, we come to interpreting the fish-eating episode in Luke 24: 42–3. As I have pointed out,[44] the other texts that Augustine had in mind or could have had in mind (Acts 1: 4; 10: 40–1; and Jn. 21: 9–14) are less clear or, at most, play only a subordinate role in supporting the conclusion that the risen Christ literally ate and drank.

With other New Testament material (Mk. 16: 14; Jn. 21), Luke 24: 42–3 recalls an appearance to a group of disciples on the occasion of their being together for a meal. But it does not follow that the risen Jesus himself quite literally ate and drank with these disciples (stage one of the tradition). In the life of the early Church (stage two of the

---

[43] For further discussion, see G. O'Collins, 'The Appearances of the Risen Christ: A Lexical-Exegetical Examination of St Paul and Other Witnesses', *Irish Theological Quarterly* 79 (2014), 128–43; reprinted in O'Collins, *Christology: Origins, Developments, Debates* (Waco, TX: Baylor University Press, 2015), 49–64.

[44] See Chapter 1, and O'Collins, *Interpreting the Resurrection* (Mahwah, NJ: Paulist Press, 1988), 39–52, 77–80.

tradition), a sacramental, Eucharistic setting may have preserved a memory of the risen Lord's encounter with the disciples when they had assembled for table-fellowship. Since it is an item shared by Luke 24: 42–3 and John 21: 1–14, fish may have featured in stage two of the tradition and concerned the remembrance of Jesus' feeding the five thousand with 'five loaves and two fishes' (Lk. 9: 16–17 parr.)—a meal told with strong Eucharistic overtones by all four evangelists.

Luke himself (stage three of the tradition) uses the fish-eating motif as one of his means for expressing at least three things: (a) the bodily reality of the risen Lord; (b) the disciples' personal experience of that reality which qualified them as reliable witnesses; and (c) the ongoing liturgical presence of the Lord. Possibly Luke 24: 42–3 is also meant to communicate (d) a sense of forgiveness and reconciliation, and (e) a call to share food in the true fellowship that hospitality requires.[45] The main thrusts of the motif are apologetic (concerning the living Jesus himself), apostolic (concerning the normative witnesses to the resurrection), and sacramental (concerning the ongoing Eucharistic life of the community). As part of his way of conveying these three points, Luke employs the fish-eating motif. He does not, however, want his readers to imagine that the risen Lord quite literally consumed (and digested) some fish before the astonished eyes of his disciples. The Christ who had already entered into glory (Lk. 24: 26) was beyond all that. What can we say about his transformed, bodily life?

The Risen, Glorious Body of Christ

A book edited by Niels Gregersen, *Incarnation: On the Scope and Depth of Christology*,[46] explored the loving outreach to all creatures on the part of God, present through the Word and the Spirit to each created being. As Gregersen himself writes, 'just as Christ the Logos is the deep bond between all that exists, so God's life-giving Spirit is moving

---

[45] Luke-Acts persistently emphasizes the hospitality of eating and drinking in fellowship; see Craig S. Keener, *Acts: An Exegetical Commentary*, ii (Grand Rapids, MI: Baker Academic, 2013), 1806.

[46] Minneapolis: Fortress Press, 2015.

all things that exist'.[47] With the incarnation, the Logos becomes an integral and central part of the whole of material reality. The earthly body of Christ inserted him into the material world; he became part of the gigantic and interrelated cosmos.

Augustine remarked that, since 'something is always leaving our bodies in a kind of continual flow or current', we need to 'recharge our strength and energy' through eating and drinking (s. 362.11).[48] Even so, Augustine could not have known how much our physical life involves a dynamic process of continual circulation between our bodies and our material environment. With millions of cells being renewed each day in the human body, our bodies incessantly share in and relate to the universe.

Modern thinkers stress the spiritual and bodily unity of human beings, our psychosomatic unity. At the same time, a certain 'dualism' remains between matter and spirit. But one should add at once that such 'dualistic' thinking about our present existence does not necessarily steer us towards a Platonic conclusion in which 'we' (as soul or spirit) are 'in' a body or 'have' a body. Speaking of our present 'matter and spirit' need not suppose that they are utterly disparate realities that, like oil and water, will not 'mix'. Given the relation to God involved in creation and incarnation, all matter has something spiritual about it. A pure materiality that would be totally unspiritual seems impossible. All the atomic material in our universe is potentially human matter, and all human matter has something spiritual about it.

Such spiritualizing of matter continually takes place through breathing, drinking, and eating. By being taken into a human body, whether that of Jesus or of anyone else, matter becomes vitally associated with the functions of a spiritual being. Obviously matter can be understood and interpreted in various ways. Nuclear physicists also know it as empty space, the field of several basic forces. Electrons and other particles appear as either mass or energy. Nevertheless, eating, drinking, breathing, and other human activities disclose another face of matter, its possibility of being spiritualized and personalized.

---

[47] 'The Extended Body of Christ: Three Dimensions of Deep Incarnation', ibid. 251.
[48] *Sermons* (341–400), 248.

Such a personalist understanding of the matter that forms the human body, also offers a personalist understanding of the body and its links with the material world and beyond. As Wilhelm Breuning put it, 'the body is man [!] insofar as, with his whole being, including his relationship towards God and his fellow men, he stands in the [material] world', which he has shaped and by which he has been shaped, 'and in this way [he] lifts the [material] world itself into the sphere of personal existence'.[49]

Against this background, one can appreciate how the resurrection of the dead, pre-eminently in the case of Jesus but also, analogously, in the case of other human beings, means the full and final personalizing and spiritualizing of our matter, not its abolition or abandonment. Through the action of the Holy Spirit, the human spirit will 'dominate' matter, in the sense that the body will clearly express and serve the glorified spirit of human beings. Accepting this requires a leap of the imagination. We can be helped to make this leap by reflecting on one aspect of risen transformation, our capacity to communicate.

Here and now our material bodiliness creates the possibility of being *communicators*. With and through our bodies we act, express ourselves, relate, and communicate with others. Without our bodies, there would be no language, no literature, no art, no religion, no industry, no political life, no social and economic relations, and none of that married love in which verbal and non-verbal communication reaches a supremely intense level. In short, without our bodies we could not make and shape our human history. Through our bodies we build up a vast web of relationships with other human beings, with the material universe, and with God. Our bodies enable us to communicate, play the human game, and compose our individual, personal stories.

Although our bodies make it possible for us to communicate, at the same time they put limits to our communication. Being subject to the constraints of space and time, our bodies set us apart and restrict our chances of relating and communicating. People talk, hug, kiss, make telephone calls, send e-mails and text messages, write letters, and in

---

[49] W. Breuning, 'Death and Resurrection in the Christian Message', in Johannes Wagner (ed.), *Reforming the Rites of Death*, *Concilium* 32 (New York: Paulist Press, 1968), 7–24, at 16–17.

other ways try to make up quantitatively for what they lack qualitatively. Through sickness, old age, imprisonment, exile, and other causes, our bodies can bring us radical solitude and terrifying loneliness. That bodily loneliness and breakdown in communication find their final expression when a tomb contains a newly buried corpse or a crematorium the fresh ashes of someone.

Few modern writers have described that irreversible break more poignantly than John McGahern, who lost his faith and then lost his devout, Irish mother when she died from cancer at the age of 42: 'She was gone. She would never answer to her name again. She was gone for ever…gone where I could not follow.'[50] When his mother Monica died at the age of 56, Augustine, her eldest child, admitted, 'my life seemed shattered, for her life and mine had been as one'. But, while she was dead, she was only 'hidden awhile from my sight', as he hoped to join both his parents through resurrection in 'the eternal Jerusalem' (*Confessions*, 11.12, 13).[51]

We may happily imagine bodily resurrection as restoring *and maximizing* our capacity to relate and communicate. The supreme example here is, of course, Jesus himself. As raised from the dead through the transforming Spirit, he now relates to the Father, human beings, and the whole cosmos in a manner that has shed the constraints of his earthly existence. Wherever two or three gather in his name, they experience the risen Lord in their midst (Matt. 18: 20). Nothing reveals more powerfully the new communicative power of Jesus than the Eucharist. It effects his worldwide presence and his offer to communicate a life that will never end.

This transformation of the dead Jesus into a new, risen mode of communicative existence is signalled by his empty tomb. It was a transformation that brought no loss of personal identity. The Easter narratives of Matthew, Luke, and John make it credible that, when the resurrected Jesus appeared to individuals and groups of disciples, they could recognize him as the same Jesus whom they had come to know during his earthly lifetime. Some (transformed) material continuity enabled them to identify the Risen One as numerically identical with

---

[50] J. McGahern, *All Will Be Well* (New York: Random House, 2007), 136, 138.

[51] Saint Augustine, *Confessions*, trans. R. S. Pine-Coffin (London: Penguin Books, 1961), 201, 203, 205.

Jesus they had known. Yet the preservation of individual, personal identity in a risen existence is not without problems.[52]

Here and now in our earthly existence, our bodies ensure our personal continuity and our being recognizable as the same person. To be and to be recognized as the same person, we must remain 'the same body'. Despite our continual and sometimes massive bodily changes, our personal continuity and identity are somehow bound up with our bodily identity and continuity. We are and have the same body, and therefore remain the same person. Bodily continuity signals the persistence of personal identity. Some thinkers (such as those who follow John Locke) have questioned the link between bodily continuity and the continuity of personal identity, understanding the latter in terms of continuity in mental states: in particular, consciousness and memories. Unquestionably, chains of conscious memories have a role in maintaining our sense of personal identity. The memory of what I have personally experienced constitutes the evidence within me of my persisting identity. Yet one's enduring personhood cannot depend simply upon one's memory. Otherwise loss of memory would entail loss of personal identity. Amnesia and dementia rebut attempts to promote memory as the (sole?) means for constituting and preserving personal continuity or the continuity of the one, unique life story that is 'me'.

Personal identity and continuity, as claimed above, remain somehow bound up with bodily continuity. In the second century, Irenaeus of Lyons applied this principle (which we saw Augustine endorsing in s. 362.10, 14[53]) to the personal identity that will be maintained in the resurrection. He asked: 'With what body will the dead rise? Certainly with the same body in which they died; otherwise those who rise would not be the same persons who previously died' (*Adversus Haereses*,

---

[52] On personal identity and continuity, see Arthur C. Danto, 'Persons', in Paul Edwards (ed.), *The Encyclopedia of Philosophy*, v (New York: Macmillan, 1967), 110–14; Terence Penelhum, 'Personal Identity', ibid. 95–107; Brian Garrett, 'Personal Identity', in Edward Craig (ed.), *Routledge Encyclopedia of Philosophy*, vii (London: Routledge, 1998), 308–14; M. F. Goodman, 'Persons', in Donald M. Borchert (ed.), *The Encyclopedia of Philosophy*, vii (Detroit: Thompson-Gale, 2006), 237–44.

[53] *Sermons* (230–272B), trans. Edmund Hill (New Rochelle, NY: New City Press, 1993), 247, 250.

5.13.1). But in what sense has Jesus risen with the same body and in what sense will we rise with the same body? What counts here as bodily sameness in individual identity?

Right in our earthly life the continuous and enormous interchange of matter between our body and our environment can make us wonder how far it is correct to speak of someone being the same body at six months before birth and then again at 6, 16, and 60. As old matter is discarded and new matter absorbed into a living body, there is a steady replacement of the matter constituting that body. How do we keep the same, numerically identical body right through our lifetime? We might suggest that the unique genetic structure, which our DNA molecules carry, maintains our body as the same body through this life. But at death, with our physical remains dispersed into the environment through the decay or burning of our corpse, how can we speak of any bodily continuity between this earthly existence and our risen life?

One answer could be found by noting the connection between 'I am my body' and 'I am my history'. Through our bodiliness, we grow in relations with other persons, with God, and with the world. Our individual history comes from our body being freely 'in relationship'. This means that in creating our personal history or allowing it to be created, our exercise of freedom is intimately connected with our bodies. We create our history by freely deciding to go (not just in our imagination but with our bodies) to places of work, study, living, and relaxation. When we arrive, we do such and such things with our bodies. Thus our bodies establish the possibility of building and shaping our personal histories. As bodies we construct our histories—from conception to death. As human beings, we experience bodily or *embodied histories*.

Here we should not ignore the fact that our bodies can be victimized bodies as well as instruments of achievement. As well as freely doing things with our bodies, we can suffer bodily against our will. The history that our bodies make is both a doing and a suffering. With our bodies we both make and suffer our history. Our resurrection will involve raising all that history of action and passion.

Thinking this way gives some credibility to understanding resurrection as our particular, embodied history being raised from the dead. In resurrection, that particular bodily history that makes up the unique story of each person will be given new life. In a mysterious, transformed fashion, their risen existence will express what they as embodied persons were and became in their earthly life. Put that way, the question and view of Irenaeus make good sense: 'With what bodily history will the dead rise? Certainly with the same bodily history, at the end of which they died; otherwise those who rise would not be the same persons who previously died.' Given the intimate connection between bodiliness and history, we can say: 'the same resurrected history means the same resurrected body'.

This proposal of mine calls for further defence. First, if I ask what has made me what I am as a unique individual, it has surely been my embodied history and not the millions of molecules that in a passing parade have at different moments constituted my particular physical existence. Second, my whole bodily history is much more 'me' than the physical body that breathes its last, say at 86 years of age. In short, it makes sense to imagine the resurrection as God bringing to a transformed, personal life the total embodied history of dead individuals and so ensuring their genuine personal continuity.

Joseph Ratzinger has written of resurrection as the stage when 'matter and spirit will belong to each other in a new and definitive fashion'.[54] Obviously what I wrote above about the progressive and final spiritualizing or personalizing of matter means agreeing with this account of resurrection. Yet I would add: in the resurrection, *bodily history* and spirit will belong to each other in a new and definitive fashion.

This approach makes good sense of what happened to Jesus, the (partial) prototype of our resurrection.[55] When he rose from the dead,

---

[54] J. Ratzinger, *Eschatology: Death and Eternal Life*, trans. Michael Waldstein and Aidan Nichols (Washington: Catholic University of America Press, 1988), 194.

[55] Here we need to speak of a 'partial' rather than a complete prototype—something that can be appreciated by reflecting on the unique quality of the corpse buried by Joseph of Arimathea. First, unlike any other corpse the world has ever seen, this was the corpse of the incarnate Son of God. His personal identity gave this body a unique dignity. Second, the body buried by Joseph was the body of the Saviour who had suffered and died on the cross to bring all men and women deliverance from evil. Such a universal saving function, which essentially involved the body of Jesus, also signalled something unique about the corpse laid in the tomb on Good Friday evening. Christ's personal identity and redemptive function

his whole life rose with him. In his risen state Jesus possesses fully his whole human story. His resurrection and glorification have made his entire life and history irrevocably present. Even if they never thought precisely of 'the irrevocable presence of Jesus' earthly history', the four evangelists wrote their Gospels out of a sense that the earthly life of Jesus had risen with him and remains indispensably significant for his followers down through the ages.

This proposal about our continuity being preserved after death through our embodied history being resurrected must face the question: how can the temporal history of individuals, fashioned through a sequence of events that extended through a stretch of time, be resurrected by God in an existence that is non-temporal but eternal? Any adequate response would need to come up with a fully argued position on time and eternity and their possible relationships and even convergence. Here Brian Leftow made a notable contribution with his *Time and Eternity*.[56] He has also defended convincingly the traditional doctrine that a timeless God became incarnate and so took on a temporal existence.[57] This is to show that divine eternity (a mode of a-temporal existence) and time are not mutually exclusive. God can be both timeless and incarnate.

Moving beyond the scope of Leftow's arguments, we can fruitfully maintain an analogy between the incarnation and the resurrection. Where the incarnation involved the timeless Son of God taking on a

---

make it plausible that, in a dramatically transformed state, his dead body should have been 'incorporated' immediately into his risen existence. Hence there would be more bodily continuity between the crucified and risen Jesus than will be the case with us. Augustine expresses this redemptive role in terms of Christ as mediator and priest, who, through his resurrection and glorification, brings the faithful into his priestly body to offer eternal worship to God. While connecting him with the other members of the *Totus Christus*, what he does also sets his resurrection (and glorification) apart from that which others hope for; see Daniel J. Jones, *Christus Sacerdos in the Preaching of St Augustine: Christ and Christian Identity* (Frankfurt: Peter Lang, 2004).

[56] Ithaca, NY: Cornell University Press, 1991.

[57] B. Leftow, 'A Timeless God Incarnate', in S. T. Davis, D. Kendall, and G. O'Collins (eds.), *The Incarnation: An Interdisciplinary Symposium on the Incarnation of the Son of God* (Oxford: Oxford University Press, 2002), 273–99.

temporal existence, resurrection from the dead involves temporal human beings (that have each been embodied in their unique history) becoming eternal, to the extent that created beings can participate in the divine attribute of eternity. On the one hand, the timeless Son of God, by becoming embodied, could develop his unique human history. In a similar but not identical way, on the other hand, the embodied historical existence of human beings can through the resurrecting power of God become eternalized.

Something of this sharing in eternity shows up already in the history of human beings. Time not only involves a succession of earlier and later events (as time moves inexorably and irreversibly on) but also has something cumulative about it. More than a mere stream of fleeting moments that disappear, time entails many things coming together and being preserved: memories in the mind, marks on our bodies, webs of persisting relationships with relatives, friends, and colleagues at work, and the rest. Likewise, and much more so, resurrected life will be a gathering up or coming together of a whole, accumulated past that will remain present to us. In resurrection, through the power of God our time and history will be summed up and completed.

My proposal about our embodied history being resurrected finds support from Caroline Walker Bynum's *The Resurrection of the Body in Western Christianity: 200–1336*.[58] She illustrates extensively the persistent conviction of many ancient Christians that resurrection would preserve for all eternity their gender, family experiences, and other characteristics and events that identified them and constituted their individual history. In particular, they rejected Gnostic-style talk about Jesus himself living 'male' but rising 'human', and, more generally, views about themselves living as male or female but rising as human, with some kind of unisex, spiritual body. Such views would detach Jesus from the particular characteristics and circumstances that helped to shape his individual history and, in effect, would deny that his particular, bodily history rose with him. In rejecting such a minimalizing view of the resurrection of Jesus and their own resurrection, rank-and-file Christians were, in effect, insisting that the whole of our history rises with us.[59]

---

[58] New York: Columbia University Press, 1995.

[59] St Gregory of Nyssa risked being incompatible with the hope of Christians when he suggested that we will rise like angels, without age or sex; for details, see

Augustine's Resurrection Faith Updated

What I am suggesting goes beyond what Bruno Niederbacher has suggested in dependence upon the views of Thomas Aquinas. The same body will rise when the same rational soul (or individual, substantial form) of a deceased human being comes to form or inform matter. In Niederbacher's words, 'if the same individual, substantial form comes to form matter, there will also be numerically the same body'.[60] What makes the risen body numerically identical with the earthly body will, in this view, be the substantial form or rational soul. Wherever and whenever this form is once again embodied, it will be the same body.

This view is attractive, not least because it moves away from a long-standing and tedious effort to find plausible ways for alleging that God somehow gathers together in the risen body some of the matter that has composed the earthly body. It could not be all the matter that during a lifetime at some point constituted the body of the deceased. If so, the risen body of someone who died, say, over the age of 20, would emerge in a giant, bloated existence. I agree with Niederbacher that the same bodily person who existed on earth will exist in the afterlife, albeit under radically transformed conditions. But what will make the risen body numerically identical with the earthly body will come from the newly embodied, individual soul existing in continuity with a previous, unique embodied existence in history. The one who will rise will be *this* bodily person, who in a complete lifetime experienced (through his or her freedom and body) a unique set of relationships upon earth. It is this continuity that will determine and preserve personal identity in the resurrection.

Augustine certainly claimed that resurrection meant (a) resurrection of 'the same body' and (b) continuity in personal identity. But he needed an updated theory to indicate how this might happen. I hope that my reflections provide some help towards understanding and interpreting both (a) and (b).

---

ibid. 83. Dante's *Divine Comedy* obviously presupposes that our total embodied history will be raised from the dead.

[60] B. Niederbacher, 'Thomas Aquinas on the Numerical Identity of the Resurrected Body', in Georg Gasser (ed.), *Personal Identity and Resurrection* (Farnham, UK: Ashgate, 2010), 145–59, at 157.

Ascension

Thus far this chapter has picked up and extended what, in its first three sections, Chapter 1 presented about Augustine's teaching on the resurrection of the crucified Jesus. The same chapter pressed on to report Augustine's teaching under four further headings: (4) the new life of Christ himself after the ascension; (5) what the risen and ascended Christ reveals and does; (6) the new life communicated to members of the *Totus Christus*; and (7) the risen and ascended Christ as minister and priest. Here 'updating' Augustine suggests limiting ourselves to the theme of the ascension, and doing so in the light of two false developments: (a) an exegetical/historical distortion of Christ's ascension, and (b) a theological neglect of the ascension.

(a) With some exegetes who write on the ascension, which they frequently term the 'exaltation' or 'assumption' of Jesus, his resurrection loses its historical edge as a specific event. Even though much of the material cited by these writers goes back to the ancient world and would have been known to Augustine, he does not appear to have come across this particular way of 'reducing' the content of the early Christian proclamation of Easter. Let us examine one recent example of this reductionism.

In *Revisiting the Empty Tomb: The Early History of Easter*,[61] Daniel A. Smith draws on a mass of 'assumption' stories from Greco-Roman and Jewish sources that are supposed to unlock the 'real' meaning of the empty tomb story in Mark 16: 1–8. Let us see some of the details.

Smith limits himself to (1) exploring the tradition of Jesus' empty tomb (as he reconstructs its religious background) and the tradition of the post-resurrection appearances, and to (2) accounting for the differences of perspective between these two traditions. He explains the differences by arguing that the empty tomb tradition did not originate as a way of stating that Jesus had been raised from the dead, but originated as a 'disappearance tradition' or a way of expressing that Jesus had been assumed from the tomb into heaven and would be seen again at the Parousia. He associates the earliest form of the disappearance tradition as he detects it in Mark 16: 1–8 with, for instance, the

[61] Minneapolis: Fortress, 2010.

disappearance of Elijah in 2 Kings 2. One might at once raise a serious doubt here. Elijah, unlike Jesus, had not been killed and buried before being assumed.

Smith has studied assiduously many ancient texts that seem relevant to his argument, along with modern authors who comment on them. He notes significant differences between Jewish accounts of assumption (through which Elijah and others escape from death by being 'taken up' with a view to their eschatological functions to come) and Greco-Roman stories. The latter usually involved an apotheosis, in which some hero was taken alive into the presence of the gods or in which his spirit ascended while his dead body was buried.

Smith acknowledges that we have something unique in the case of Jesus: Christian belief in him involved *both* resurrection *and* assumption/ascension (e.g. Phil. 2: 9; 1 Tim. 3: 16). But he never acknowledges a key difficulty thrown up by the cases he cites of Heracles, Romulus, and other such heroes and heroines. Unlike Jesus (who lived and died shortly before the New Testament came into existence) these heroes and heroines were understood to have lived in a very distant past, and—one can reasonably maintain—most probably never existed at all. A similar difficulty also affects the way in which Elijah and other ancient biblical figures might be pressed into service as parallels for the traditions that arose about what happened to Jesus. Whatever one's verdict on the historical reality of these ancient figures, they certainly did not exist, as Jesus did, within living memory.

Smith does not refer to Richard Bauckham's *Jesus and the Eyewitnesses: The Gospels as Eyewitness Testimony*,[62] a work that might have curbed his willingness to credit the New Testament authors and their sources with a high degree of 'creativity'. Bauckham recognizes that the period between Jesus and the final composition of Mark and the other Gospels was spanned by the continued presence and testimony of some who had participated in the history of Jesus: namely, such eyewitnesses as Peter, Andrew, Mary Magdalene, and the sons of Zebedee. They played a central and authoritative role in guiding the transmission of traditions about Jesus, and would not have tolerated 'creative' innovations. Bauckham's reconstruction of the function

---

[62] Grand Rapids, MI: Eerdmans, 2006.

of the original eyewitnesses does not allow for the kind of imaginative developments Smith alleges. On the basis of a saying from Q (a collection of sayings of Jesus), 'you will not see me' (Matt. 23: 39; Lk. 13: 35), Smith imagines Mark and/or his sources fashioning an empty tomb tradition that involved Jesus not being raised from the dead but being taken up into heaven and no longer 'seen'.

Smith offers various helpful insights when treating details in the Easter chapters of Luke and Matthew. But the arguments in favour of his central theme (that, as we move from Mark to John, we see a progressive accommodation of a disappearance/assumption tradition, first found in Mark, to an appearance/resurrection tradition) fail to convince, and that for at least three strong reasons.

First, the Greco-Roman material used to support Smith's interpretation of Mark 16: 1–8 as a disappearance/assumption story seems largely irrelevant to a Gospel that most scholars interpret against a Jewish background. This evangelist sets the story of Jesus within Jewish salvation history; his text is permeated with quotation from and echoes of the Jewish scriptures, as he goes about illustrating how Jesus fulfilled various Jewish motifs. Greco-Roman motifs do not provide a key, let alone a master key, for interpreting what Mark wrote either in his last chapter or in the rest of his Gospel. In a literary and rhetorical study of this Gospel, Paul Danove finds little or no evidence of Greco-Roman influence.[63] Years ago, in a paper that anticipated the thesis of Smith's book, Adela Yarbro Collins 'explained' Mark's empty tomb story largely on the basis of Greco-Roman ideas of a notable figure being translated into heaven. Yet she had to admit that 'it is hard to find' in Mark much influence from Greco-Roman sources.[64]

---

[63] P. L. Danove, *The End of Mark's Story: A Methodological Study* (Leiden: Brill, 1993).

[64] A. Yarbro Collins, 'The Empty Tomb in the Gospel According to Mark', in Eleonore Stump and Thomas P. Flint (eds.), *Hermas and Athena* (Notre Dame, IN: University of Notre Dame Press, 1993), 107–40, at 130–1. In her *Mark: A Commentary* (Minneapolis: Fortress, 2007), she wrote of 'the possibility of the influence on Mark 16: 1–8 of ancient notions of the translation or transference of a body of a favoured person to the ends of the earth or to heaven, where he or she is made immortal. Ancient notions of deification or apotheosis may also have influenced the story of the empty tomb.' She concluded: 'The author of Mark

Second, as we move from Mark to John, we do find a progressive linking of two traditions. But it is a progression that links the tradition of the discovery of the empty tomb (entailing Jesus' resurrection from the dead, not his assumption into heaven) with the tradition of his appearances. Thus Mark 16: 1–8 reports the tomb of Jesus being discovered open and empty, a promise of one or more appearances in Galilee, but no actual appearance of the resurrected Jesus. By the time we reach John 20, we read not only of the discovery of the empty tomb but also of an appearance (to Mary Magdalene) right at the tomb itself.

Third, the central statement in the Easter chapter of Mark is 'he was raised' from the dead (along with 'he is going before you into Galilee and there you will see him'), not 'he has been taken up into heaven' (and 'you will see him again at the Parousia'). Smith tries hard to explain (or explain away) Mark's text in favour of his disappearance/assumption thesis. But the arguments seem contrived. The language of assumption or ascension turns up elsewhere in the New Testament (e.g. Phil. 2: 9; 1 Tim. 3: 16) but not in Mark 16: 1–8. Smith's thesis looks like a thorough distortion. If he had come across such a distortion, Augustine might well have said: 'Now resurrection is swallowed up in exaltation. O resurrection, where is your victory? O resurrection, where is your sting?'

(b) Chapter 1 showed how belief in the ascension was integral to Augustine's picture of the glorified Christ mediating new life to believers. Against Donatist views, which played down the primary role of Christ as mediator and priest, Augustine insisted on the risen and ascended Christ being the only true minister of the sacraments, who also eternally offers his sacrifice on our behalf. Following Romans 8: 34 and Hebrews 7: 25, Augustine portrayed Christ 'established in heaven', where as king he reigns over us and as priest 'intercedes for

---

was probably aware of the idea that some Roman emperors had ascended into heaven and become gods. He may also have known that their deification was modelled on that of Romulus' (pp. 791–2, 793). No evidence is cited to show any such 'awareness' on the part of the evangelist: what was stated as 'possible' becomes 'probable'—once again without any evidence being produced.

us' (en. Ps. 19.10).[65] The continual heavenly intercession, made possible by the resurrection and ascension, summarizes the eternal, priestly work of Christ. In one of his recently discovered sermons, we find Augustine proclaiming that 'it is the whole universal Church which is the body of that one priest' (s. 198.49).[66] The risen and ascended/glorified Christ presents to God one priestly body as an eternal offering of worship.

Any theology of the sacraments will remain impoverished unless it follows Augustine in reflecting on the risen *and ascended* Christ being the primary minister of the sacraments. Any theology of the priesthood will likewise remain impoverished unless it follows Romans, Hebrews, and Augustine by incorporating the eternal intercession of the ascended and high-priestly Christ. Anthony Kelly has recently protested against a widespread neglect of the ascension among Western theologians and the loss it brings to their theology.[67] This neglect has gone hand in hand with a neglect of the Letter to the Hebrews and a corresponding neglect of Christ's eternal priesthood.

A generation ago, a shining exception came from Thomas F. Torrance in his reflections on the work of Christ as priest and mediator. He wrote: the Eucharist 'is Christ himself who is really present pouring out his Spirit upon us' and 'uniting us with his self-oblation and self-presentation before the face of the Father where he ever lives to make intercession for us'.[68] Inasmuch as he took on the human condition, the resurrected and ascended Christ could continue forever his function as Priest and Mediator between God the Father and human beings.

---

[65] *Expositions of the Psalms* (1–32), trans. Maria Boulding (Hyde Park, NY: New City Press, 2000), 216–17.

[66] *Newly Discovered Sermons*, trans. Edmund Hill (Hyde Park, NY: New City Press, 1997), 218.

[67] A. Kelly, *Upward: Faith, Church, and the Ascension of Christ* (Collegeville, MN: Liturgical Press, 2014).

[68] T. F. Torrance, *Theology in Reconciliation: Essays Toward Evangelical and Catholic Unity in East and West* (London: Geoffrey Chapman, 1975), 118. On Torrance's understanding of Christ's eternal priesthood, see further G. O'Collins and M. K. Jones, *Jesus Our Priest: A Christian Approach to the Priesthood of Christ* (Oxford: Oxford University Press, 2010), 224–9.

Even though his patristic heroes are different, Torrance valued Augustine for what he taught on the mediatorial work of Christ, a work made possible insofar as he was truly man.[69] It was the incarnation that eventually (through resurrection and ascension) enabled Christ to become the High Priest eternally interceding in heaven.

This chapter has attempted to retrieve and update for today Augustine's doctrinal teaching on Christ's resurrection. What remains is the task of 'updating' his rhetorical apologetic for that resurrection.

---

[69] Torrance, *Theology in Reconciliation*, 194.

4
Augustine's Case for the Resurrection Updated

Chapter 2 charted the rhetorical 'apology' that Augustine constructed for believing in the risen Jesus, a commitment that he understood to establish the identity of Christians. In justifying faith in the resurrection, he appealed to the divine power already shown in created nature, to historical evidence, and to his audience's deep hunger for lasting happiness. Their feelings, along with creation and history, entered into the cumulative argument he put together. We recognized some places where modern scholars parallel Augustine's approach: for instance, in arguments from observable effects to the only adequate cause being the resurrection of Jesus (e.g. Hans Küng, Richard Swinburne, and N. T. Wright) and the hunger of the human heart for the fullness of lasting life that the resurrection promises (Karl Rahner).[1] We also took stock of Augustine's 'failure' to reflect on the appearances of the risen Christ and the empty tomb. This chapter singles out four areas that should loom large when we set ourselves to update Augustine's apology for the resurrection: the marvellous nature of creation; the appearances of the risen Jesus; the discovery of the open and empty tomb; and 'going beyond' the evidence in coming to Easter faith.

---

[1] While paralleling Augustine's effect-cause argument, Küng, Swinburne, and Wright do not seem aware of this. Rahner, however, here and there engaged with Augustine. Rahner and Augustine converge, for instance, in their stress on the experience of God and what Rahner called 'the divine self-communication' to the heart of all human beings. See B. Kleinschwärzer-Meister, 'Rahner, Karl', in Karla Pollmann (ed.), *The Oxford Guide to the Historical Reception of Augustine*, iii (Oxford: Oxford University Press, 2013), 1635–8.

The Marvellous Nature of Creation

Augustine's faith in God as the Creator of the world proved essential in his 'apology' for the resurrection of Jesus from the dead. The God of the original creation does not lack means when it comes to the new creation or raising the dead to new life—even raising aborted foetuses and human beings eaten by wild beasts or cannibals (civ. 22.13, 20).[2] The innumerable marvels that fill the world provided Augustine with further reasons for holding that God can raise the dead and, in fact, has raised Jesus from the dead (civ. 21.9).[3] He cited, for instance, 'the daily miracle' of babies growing in their mothers' wombs and being born every day. God who brings us forth 'in proper shape from the womb' can also bring us alive 'from the tomb' (s. 242A.2).[4] Augustine marvelled also at the 'new life after death' that the season of spring brings after winter (s. 361.10).[5]

If Augustine had lived much later and cast his eye over the case for all living things being descended through a very long, evolutionary process from a common ancestor, he would have been even more astonished at the amazing world in which we exist. He would have found the mystery that still shrouds the 'how' of life's origins intriguing. Life did not have to appear and evolve; the probability of life, so scientists assure us, was close to zero.[6] Like Francis S. Collins (b. 1950), the geneticist who led the Human Genome Project and from 2009 has been the director of the National Institutes of Health, Augustine would surely have found evolution enhancing his appreciation of God's creative work. Yet it is not merely evolutionary theory

---

[2] *The City of God XI–XXII*, trans. William Babcock (Hyde Park, NY: New City Press, 2013), 524 and 530–1.

[3] Ibid. 464.

[4] *Sermons* (230–272B), trans. Edmund Hill (New Rochelle, NY: New City Press, 1993), 86.

[5] *Sermons* (341–400), trans. Edmund Hill (New Rochelle, NY: New City Press, 1995), 231.

[6] On the origins of life, see John C. Lennox, *God's Undertaker: Has Science Buried God?* (Oxford: Lion, 2007), 116–26; and Alistair E. McGrath, *A Fine-Tuned Universe: The Quest for God in Science and Theology* (Louisville, KY: Westminster John Knox, 2009), 127–42.

that would have given a new edge to Augustine's wonder at creation. Modern astronomy, physics, chemistry, and biology have revealed innumerable astonishing facts about the whole universe and the earth on which we live. Increased wonder at the workings of nature has led many scientists and philosophers of science to a richer sense of God the Creator, and can predispose them to accept belief in the new creation that was Christ's resurrection from the dead and that will come to all human beings and their world.[7]

Gerard Manley Hopkins (1844–89) was in line with Augustine when he wrote: 'the world is charged with the grandeur of God'. In his sonnet 'God's Grandeur' he confronted a problem that Augustine repeatedly remarked on: the marvels of the created world are so common that they are often 'disregarded as uninteresting' (s. 242.1).[8] Constant experience can have a dulling effect, and needs to be counteracted by attending to the discoveries of modern scientists, the insights of poets, or the deep appreciation of nature coming from other people. Only those who feel some wonder at our marvellous world will be open to hear the message of the resurrection. A dull failure to be astonished by the extraordinary aspects of the first creation can fatally narrow any openness to reckon with the even more extraordinary event which has inaugurated the new creation, Jesus' glorious resurrection from the dead.

To sum up. Augustine rightly held that, without accepting God as all-powerful and all-loving, one could not entertain the notion of the dead being brought from death to new life. He also recognized that those who lack all sense of wonder at God's original creation will need to change if they are to accept the message of Easter faith.

---

[7] See the scientists and philosophers of science who contributed to Gerald O'Collins and Mary Ann Myers (eds.), *Light from Light: Scientists and Theologians in Dialogue* (Grand Rapids, MI: Eerdmans, 2012); to Ted Peters, Robert J. Russell, and Michael Welker (eds.), *Resurrection: Theological and Scientific Assessments* (Grand Rapids, MI: Eerdmans, 2002); and to Robert J. Russell, William R. Stoeger, and Francisco J. Ayala (eds.), *Evolutionary and Molecular Biology: Scientific Perspectives on Divine Action* (Berkeley, CA: Center for Theology and Natural Sciences, 1998).

[8] *Sermons* (230–272B), 78.

Interpreting and Defending the Appearances

As we recalled in Chapter 2 (n. 6), Augustine had read the late third-century Neoplatonist, Porphyry. But he did not challenge—probably he did not know—the way Porphyry cast doubt on the appearances of the risen Jesus by noting their non-public character. This philosopher argued that if the risen Christ had truly appeared risen from the dead, he should have made himself known to his Jewish opponents, to Pilate and Herod, and, even better, to the members of the Roman Senate (*Against the Christians: The Literary Remains*).[9]

A century earlier than Porphyry, Celsus had made the same objection: 'if [the risen] Jesus really wanted to show forth divine power, he ought to have appeared to the very men who treated him despitefully and to the man [Pilate] who condemned him and to everyone everywhere' (*Contra Celsum* 2.63).[10]

Many centuries later Hermann Reimarus (1694–1768) declared the lack of such public appearances to be irreconcilable with Jesus' alleged mission to call all people to a new faith. 'If only he had manifested himself one single time after his resurrection in the temple, before the people and the Sanhedrin in Jerusalem, visibly, audibly, tangibly', Reimarus wrote, 'then it could not fail that the entire Jewish nation would have believed in him'. Hence Reimarus concluded: 'even if we had no other stumbling block about Jesus' resurrection, this single one, that he would not allow himself to be seen publicly, would itself be enough to throw all its credibility aside, because it cannot agree in all eternity with Jesus' intention in coming into the world'.[11]

Against Porphyry, Celsus, and Reimarus, one might retort that, given the new status of the risen Christ as constituting the beginning of the end of the world (1 Cor. 15: 20, 23), those who saw him needed to be offered and to receive some graced powers of perception. Seeing the risen Christ required some transforming grace for the recipients of

---

[9] Trans. R. Joseph Hoffmann (Amherst, NY: Prometheus Books, 1994), 34.

[10] From Celsus, *True Discourse*, cited by Origen in *Contra Celsum*, trans. Henry Chadwick, *Origen Contra Celsum*, rev. edn. (Cambridge: Cambridge University Press, 1965), 114.

[11] *Reimarus Fragments*, no. 32, ed. C. H. Talbert, trans. R. S. Fraser (Philadelphia: Fortress, 1970), 199–200.

that experience. They had to be made in some sense like him, a grace that was not given to, or at least not received by, the guards at the tomb or by Paul's companions on the road to Damascus. The former were 'shaken by fear' of the angel of the Lord and 'became like dead men' (Matt. 28: 4), The latter are described as 'hearing the voice but seeing no one' (Acts 9: 7), 'seeing the light but not hearing the voice' (Acts 22: 9), and 'falling to the ground' with Paul (Acts 26: 14). The guards and Paul's companions remained mere observers; they did not become graced participants.

Augustine had almost nothing to say about expounding and defending the post-resurrection appearances. Since he paid so little attention to what seeing the risen Christ entailed, there is no question of simply refashioning the teaching of Augustine. Apropos of the Easter appearances, it needs to be supplemented, even beyond what Chapter 3 has already offered.

The New Testament reports that, after his death and burial, various individuals and groups saw Jesus gloriously alive. He appeared

- To 'the twelve' (1 Cor. 15: 5)
- To 'the eleven and those with them' (Lk. 24: 33–49)
- To 'those who came up with him [Jesus] from Galilee' (Acts 13: 31)
- To 'the disciples' (Mk. 16: 7; Jn. 20: 19–23)
- To 'all the apostles' (1 Cor. 15: 7; a distinct and larger group than 'the twelve')
- To Simon Peter and six other 'disciples' (Jn. 21: 1–14)
- To 'more than five hundred brothers and sisters' (1 Cor. 15: 6)
- To Cleopas and his companion (Lk. 24: 13–35)
- To Mary Magdalene and 'the other Mary' (Matt. 28: 9–10)
- To Mary Magdalene (Jn. 20: 11–18; Mk.16: 9–11)
- To Cephas/Peter (1 Cor. 15: 5; Mk. 16: 7; Lk. 24: 34)
- To James (1 Cor. 15: 7)
- To Saul/Paul (e.g. 1 Cor. 9: 1; 15: 8; Acts 9: 1–9).

This and further testimony to the appearances of the risen Jesus (e.g. Acts 1: 3–5; 10: 40–2) can diverge on secondary matters. Who was the first to see him? Mary Magdalene or Simon Peter? Where did these appearances take place—in Galilee (e.g. Mk 16: 7) or in and around Jerusalem (Lk. 24)? Yet the sources agree on the primary fact of appearances to certain individuals and to groups, in particular, to the core group of disciples, 'the twelve' (e.g. 1 Cor. 15: 5).

In the light of what Chapter 3 presented about the post-resurrection 'Christophanies', supplemented by the fuller argument in the *Irish Theological Quarterly*,[12] we can sum up the New Testament witness. Despite a certain ordinariness about the Easter appearances (which led Mary Magdalene into thinking the risen Jesus was a gardener, Jn. 20: 15), the New Testament attributes (1) a transformed life to him. His new embodied existence is no longer subject to the normal limitations of the material universe; he now exists 'beyond' and 'lives to God' (Rom. 6: 10). Yet (2) he freely emerged from the other world to enter into contact with people of this world (both individuals and groups), (3) revealing himself to them (e.g. Gal. 1: 1, 12, 15–16), (4) calling them to faith and mission (e.g. 1 Cor. 9: 1), and (5) doing so in a way that included a certain kind of external perception or visual component. For some people, point (5) creates difficulties and calls for further comment.

With the Easter encounters we are dealing with claims about a bodily resurrected person letting himself be seen by persons who exist in our space-time world. It is difficult to imagine how a purely spiritual, interior seeing could be reconciled with the New Testament terminology of the appearances. This is not to argue, however, that when the risen Jesus appeared he was an exterior object to be perceived or recognized by anyone who happened to be present, irrespective of their personal dispositions.

Yet one must admit that Paul and the evangelists show little interest in describing, let alone explaining in detail, the nature of the appearances. I simply want to point out that some visible component seems implied by the language that the New Testament uses for the encounters with the risen Jesus. Unlike the Old Testament prophets, the apostolic witnesses to the resurrection typically saw the risen Lord rather than heard him.

---

[12] G. O'Collins, 'The Appearances of the Risen Christ: A Lexical-Exegetical Examination of St Paul and Other Witnesses', *Irish Theological Quarterly* 79 (2014), 128–43; reprinted in O'Collins, *Christology: Origins, Developments, Debates* (Waco, TX: Baylor University Press, 2015), 49–64.

Here, of course, we should recall that the New Testament often fills out 'seeing' with a meaning that includes but goes beyond a merely literal and everyday sense. When Jesus 'saw' Simon and his brother Andrew and then 'saw' the sons of Zebedee (Mk. 1: 16, 19), it was a significant look. The connotations of 'calling' were close at hand; that was true also in the case of Jesus' seeing Levi (Lk. 5: 27 parr.). The desire of Zacchaeus to see Jesus (Lk. 19: 3–4) likewise included but went beyond mere physical perception, and seemed to hint at the way in which the tax collector already half sensed that Jesus could bring him salvation. Zacchaeus' eagerness to see Jesus was no 'mere expression of curiosity' but 'something more', a 'vague discernment of something special about this person who was passing through and of whom he had heard'.[13] Add too the way 'seeing' in John's Gospel includes but goes beyond its simple, everyday meaning, so as to suggest a passage to faith (e.g. Jn. 1: 39; 12: 21). 'Seeing' is almost synonymous with 'believing' (e.g. Jn. 9: 37–8). 'Opening the eyes' (seven times in Jn. 9: 1–41) is tantamount to being brought to believe. Faith, to quote Augustine, is a seeing 'with the eyes of the heart' (s. 263.3) or an 'inner gazing of the heart' (s. 264.2).[14]

Since 'seeing' could enjoy this richer sense during the story of Jesus' ministry, we should all the more insist that normal, everyday perception by itself does not do justice to what 'seeing' the risen Lord entailed (e.g. Jn. 20: 28; 1 Cor. 9: 1). That 'seeing' included but rose above mere visual perception.

Since the second century, the objective reality of the post-resurrection appearances of Jesus has been questioned. As we saw in Chapters 2 and 3, Celsus, a pagan philosopher in the oldest literary attack on Christianity, argued that an alleged witness to the risen Jesus was hysterical and hallucinated (Mary Magdalene) and in the case of 'some other one' (presumably Peter) either hallucinated or was an ambitious liar: he 'either dreamt in a certain state of mind and through wishful thinking had an hallucination…or, what is more likely, wanted to impress the others by telling this fantastic tale'.[15] By branding Mary

---

[13] Joseph A. Fitzmyer, *The Gospel According to Luke X–XXIV* (New York: Doubleday, 1985), 1223.

[14] *Sermons* (230–272B), 220, 227.

[15] From Celsus' *True Discourse*, cited by Origen in *Contra Celsum* (2.55), trans. Chadwick, 109.

Magdalene as a hysterical woman, Celsus began a long tradition of gratuitously alleging that the disciples of Jesus, both male and female, were temperamental, even unbalanced by character and prone to visions. Every now and then they continue to be depicted this way, even though there is not a shred of evidence that they were more prone to be hallucinated than anyone else.

Augustine did not know the objection coming from Celsus, or at least he did not take it up. But the challenge continues. In modern times various writers have dismissed the post-resurrection appearances as experiences of hallucinated persons who, after Jesus' death and burial, were anxiously expecting to see him risen from the dead and, through a kind of chain reaction, mistakenly imagined that they saw him present to them. They attributed to an external source what they had thought up for themselves: the 'presence' of the risen Christ. Thus Gerd Lüdemann developed the hallucination theory and other claims about the psychohistory of Peter and Paul.[16] Lüdemann is yet another example of a non-medical writer offering psychiatric explanations that would never be accepted by a peer-reviewed medical journal.[17]

The evidence that we have from the four Gospels does not support a picture of Jesus' disciples excitedly expecting to meet him risen from the dead. Instead of persuading themselves into thinking they saw him, they had to be persuaded that he was gloriously alive again (e.g. Lk. 24: 36–43; Jn. 20: 24–5). What the Gospels report seems credible: the tragic crisis of Jesus' arrest and disgraceful death on a cross left the disciples crushed. Only by ignoring the evidence can we picture them anxiously awaiting his return from the dead and out of their imagination hallucinating the appearances.

Furthermore, hallucinations are private, individual experiences, and do not fit the disciples' group encounters with the risen Jesus. Of course, the thesis of an ecstatic group hallucination might be more plausible if the New Testament had reported only one appearance of

---

[16] G. Lüdemann, *The Resurrection of Jesus*, trans. John Bowden (Minneapolis: Fortress, 1994); see my reviews of that book in *Gregorianum* 77 (1996), 357–9, and *Theological Studies* 57 (1996), 341–3.

[17] See Joseph W. Bergeron and Gary R. Habermas, 'The Resurrection of Jesus: A Clinical Review of Psychiatric Hypotheses for the Biblical Story of Easter', *Irish Theological Quarterly* 80 (2015), 157–72.

the risen Christ and that to a particular group on a particular day. Instead, it witnesses to appearances over a period of time and to different groups as well as to different individuals (e.g. Cephas/Peter, James, and Paul in 1 Cor. 15: 5, 7–8). As regards the groups, the New Testament testimony presents us with at least seven distinct groups: the 'twelve' (1 Cor. 15: 5); 'all the apostles' (1 Cor. 15: 7); 'the eleven and their companions' (Lk. 24: 23); Simon Peter and six others (Jn. 21: 1–14); 'more than five hundred brothers and sisters' (1 Cor. 15: 6); Cleopas and his companion (Lk. 24: 13–35); and Mary Magdalene and 'the other Mary' (Matt. 28: 9–10). The variety of traditions makes it quite implausible to reduce these seven groups to one group who, on a particular occasion and by a kind of chain reaction, imagined one after another that they saw Jesus. In short, the hallucination hypothesis offers a psychological explanation but cannot produce historical evidence in support of such an explanation.

What of Paul? Did he deceive himself into thinking he saw the risen Christ? As has been repeatedly observed, the hypothesis of a group hallucination fails to account for the case of Paul. Far from hoping to meet the risen Jesus, he persecuted the first Christians. His encounter with Christ (1 Cor. 9: 1; 15: 8; Gal. 1: 12, 16; Acts 9: 1–9) took place several years later and in a different place from the other Easter appearances (Galilee and in or near Jerusalem). Before the meeting on the Damascus road, Paul was in no way committed to Jesus. Quite the contrary! The appearance to Paul could not be a case of wish fulfilment.

Yet might it be that his persecution of the Christians disclosed a deep conflict within him, a 'Christ complex' that finally resolved itself when he hallucinated the presence of Christ?[18] But do we have any reliable evidence that might let us enter into the consciousness of Paul *before* his Damascus road experience? Years later and with extreme brevity, Paul recalled how, when he persecuted the Church, he was blameless and righteous from the standpoint of the law (Phil. 3: 6; Gal. 1: 13–14). Here Lüdemann seems out of date in his approach. Most historians now view with scepticism attempts to psychoanalyse people

---

[18] Lüdemann, *Resurrection of Jesus*, 79–84.

long dead, especially someone like the younger Paul, about whose interior, mental life we lack data. He left us little information about his emotional and mental state as a Christian and nothing at all about that state in his pre-Christian days.

Before leaving the persistent claim about hallucination, let us return to the first disciples of Jesus and note three difficulties with this claim. Any hallucination hypothesis depends upon (a) what they *already* believed and (b) what they *already* expected. Such a hypothesis may also (c) appeal to 'bereavement' experiences or cases of bereaved people who experience their beloved dead.

(a) The first disciples, soon after his death and burial, began preaching the crucified Jesus as the divinely endorsed Messiah risen from the dead to bring salvation to all people. The notion of a Messiah who failed, suffered, was crucified, and then rose from the grave was simply foreign to pre-Christian Judaism and could not have shaped any hallucinations on the part of the earliest (Jewish) disciples.[19] This was not a prior, religious belief which might have prompted the first disciples into preaching what they did.

(b) A second (similar) problem for any hallucination hypothesis concerns a striking shift in religious expectations. By the time of Jesus some or even many Jews cherished a hope that the resurrection of all the dead and a general judgement would terminate human history.[20] But then the (Jewish) followers of Jesus began announcing that one individual had already been raised to a glorious existence that anticipated the end of all history. This remarkable change in expectations had no precedent in Jewish faith, which might have fed into alleged hallucinations on the part of the disciples. It had to have a different cause, with the only plausible candidate being the resurrection of Jesus and his Easter appearances.

(c) A third challenge to the Easter appearances has come from those who have drawn on the ground-breaking research initiated by Dewi Rees into cases of bereaved people who experienced their beloved

---

[19] In Chapter 2, we discussed more fully this religious novelty, as well as the novelty we consider under (b).

[20] See N. T. Wright, *The Resurrection of the Son of God* (London: SPCK, 2003), 146–206.

dead—by seeing them, hearing them, and so forth.[21] Some (such as Lüdemann) who have endorsed this approach allege that the Easter 'appearances' were nothing more than ancient episodes in the psychobiographies of bereaved persons.[22]

The difficulty about making much of this bereavement research comes from the numerous points of dissimilarity that militate against recognizing any close analogy between the experiences of Jesus' disciples and those of the widows and widowers studied by Rees and others. There is simply no close analogy that might prove illuminating. First, the widows and widowers who experienced their beloved dead were all individuals; Rees and his successors did not come up with any such 'group experiences'; in the case of the resurrection witness in the New Testament, the appearances of Christ to groups were at least as significant as the appearances to individuals. Second, 40 per cent of the widows and widowers studied by Rees continued to experience their deceased spouses for many years. The appearances of the risen Jesus to individuals and groups took place over a limited period of time, and did not continue for years. Third, prior to Rees's study, only 27.7 per cent of the bereaved who experienced their dead spouses had mentioned these experiences to others. The rest (72.3 per cent) had kept their experiences to themselves. Those to whom Jesus appeared (Peter, Mary Magdalene, and so on) joyfully passed on to others the good news of the resurrection. Readers who are interested can read what I have written about further points of dissimilarity that prevent the bereavement experiences from being anything like an illuminating or close analogy to the disciples' experiences of the risen Christ.[23]

So much of what Augustine wrote and preached on the resurrection of Jesus remains instructive and relevant. But many centuries have

---

[21] See G. O'Collins, 'The Resurrection and Bereavement Experiences', *Irish Theological Quarterly* 76 (2011), 224–37; reprinted in O'Collins, *Believing in the Resurrection: The Meaning, and Promise of the Risen Jesus* (Mahwah, NJ: Paulist Press, 2012), 175–91.

[22] Apparently so too does Dale Allison, *Resurrecting Jesus: The Earliest Christian Tradition and Its Interpreters* (New York and London: T. & T. Clark, 2005); on Allison, see O'Collins, *Believing in the Resurrection*, 12–16.

[23] See n. 21 above.

passed. In the modern world, we need to enrich his teaching by adding the kind of considerations we have just offered on the interpretation and defence of the post-resurrection appearances of the risen Jesus. Nowadays Augustine could allow such reflections to enter his sermons and letters and even become part of a major, new work he might write, *De Resurrectione Christi* (On the Resurrection of Christ). He would likewise need to do something similar in arguing for both the historicity and theological significance of Jesus' empty tomb. It would not be enough, apropos of one (Mary Magdalene in Jn. 20: 1–2) or more women (three women in Mk. 16: 1–8) discovering the tomb to be open and empty, to state simply that the Gospels are 'supremely truthful books' (civ. 22.8).[24]

The Historicity and Significance of the Empty Tomb

From the Gospel of Matthew, Augustine knew and ridiculed a major counter-explanation proposed to account for the empty tomb: when the guards fell asleep, the disciples of Jesus quietly removed his body.[25] This or similar counter-explanations have persisted right down to the present; Chapter 3 has discussed a modern version coming from Philip Pullman. Chapter 3 also noted how Daniel Smith alleged that Mark and/or his sources, on the basis of a saying from Q, made up an empty tomb tradition that was then accepted by the other evangelists. We also recalled how Adela Yarbro Collins had already 'explained' Mark 16: 1–8 as created by the evangelist on the basis of Greco-Roman ideas of notable figures being translated into heaven. This theory denies historical status to the discovery of the empty tomb and turns it into a fictional scenario initiated, or at least encouraged, by Mark. Nowadays Augustine would need to confront such challenges to the historicity of the empty tomb of Jesus.

First, despite the theological insights and allusions that scholars have detected in the Gospel of Mark, he does not seem to have been

---

[24] *City of God XI–XII*, trans. Babcock, 505.
[25] See Chapter 3, n. 32.

very creative from a literary point of view.[26] Hence it is hardly to be expected that he would invent out of nothing not only an entire episode (the discovery of the empty tomb) but also an episode that centred on something of supreme importance, the resurrection of Jesus from the dead. Joel Marcus, while allowing for some editorial additions made by Mark (e.g. Mk. 16: 7), argues that the evangelist incorporates 'an existing narrative' into his final chapter. Marcus also draws attention to the independent witness of John 20: 1–2, which 'tells the same basic story, and in a way that is in some respects more primitive (e.g., one woman rather than three, no angelic interpreter)'.[27]

Second, the thesis that Mark ends his Gospel with a fictional story involves portraying Matthew and Luke as gullible. They use, as the majority of scholars rightly maintain, Mark 16: 1–8 as a major source when composing their Easter narratives. Matthew and Luke repeat the main lines of Mark's story about the discovery of the empty tomb as if it were a factual narrative. Have they misunderstood Mark and read as history what was intended only as an imaginative fiction about an apotheosis of Jesus? Can a modern scholar claim to evaluate better than those two evangelists the status of a main source they employ?

Third, the period between Jesus (crucified about 30 AD) and the final composition of Mark's Gospel (late 60s) was spanned by the presence and testimony of those who had participated as eyewitnesses.[28] Mark's closing chapter mentions a number of these witnesses: (1) the protagonists at the tomb, who were Mary Magdalene, Mary the mother of James (this James being presumably 'James the younger' or 'the small' mentioned by Mk. 15: 40), and Salome, and (2) those who were directed to Galilee and saw the risen Jesus—namely, Peter and other disciples. These followers of Jesus played a central role in transmitting traditions about him; some, or even many of them, were still alive in the 60s. Presumably they would not have tolerated a major innovation such as a purely fictional story of three women discovering the tomb of Jesus to be open and empty on the third

---

[26] See Joel Marcus, *Mark 1–8* (New Haven: Yale University Press, 1999), 59–62.

[27] J. Marcus, *Mark 8–16* (New Haven: Yale University Press, 2009), 1083.

[28] See what was said in Chapter 3 about Smith's failure to address this issue of eyewitnesses.

day. It is hard to imagine that Mark exposed himself to an easy rebuttal of his fiction by putting a number of eyewitnesses into his new story.

Fourth, Yarbro Collins and Smith, as we saw in Chapter 3, claim that Mark created the empty tomb episode on the basis of Greco-Roman myths of notable figures being translated into heaven. But many scholars find little or no evidence of such Greco-Roman influences either in the final chapter of Mark or in the rest of his Gospel. Such influences do not supply a master key for explaining Mark's text. Rather he set his account of Jesus within the framework of God's saving work for the chosen people. Hence he began his story by quoting Isaiah to indicate that what immediately followed (about John the Baptist) continued what God had already done: 'See I am sending my messenger ahead of you, who will prepare your way: the voice of one crying in the wilderness, "Prepare the way of the Lord; make his paths straight"' (Mk. 1: 2–3).

Fifth, apologists for a core historicity in the empty tomb stories have frequently argued from the central place of women in these stories. In the oldest version (Mk. 16: 1–8), three women were astonished to find Jesus' tomb open and empty on the first Easter Sunday morning. If this story were merely a legend created by Mark or other early Christians, they would presumably have attributed the discovery of the empty tomb to male disciples rather than to women. In first-century Palestine, women and slaves were for all intents and purposes disqualified as valid witnesses. The natural thing for someone making up a story about the empty tomb would have been to ascribe the discovery to men and not to women. Legend makers do not normally invent positively unhelpful material. Why would anyone attribute to women the key testimony to the empty tomb unless that was actually the case?

Sixth, we have no evidence that any first-century Jews (or Christians) ever embraced a belief in resurrection which did not involve the body that had been buried. Of course, there were some who accepted the kind of glorious transformation indicated by Daniel 12, and others who thought of resurrection in a material way, as the earthly body being reassembled or reconstructed (e.g. 2 Macc. 7). Nevertheless, despite their differences, all who expected resurrection agreed that the bodies in the graves would be involved when the dead were raised to new life. They neither imagined nor anticipated a personal resurrection that did not include the bodies that had been buried. For first-century Jews, no empty tomb meant no resurrection.

Such first-century beliefs support the conclusion that, at least in Jerusalem and Palestine, it would have been impossible to proclaim the resurrection of Jesus unless his tomb was known to be empty. His alleged resurrection would have been dismissed out of hand as blatantly untrue, if his tomb was known to have still contained his mortal remains.

Yet debates about the historical status of the empty tomb of Jesus do not, I believe, reach the heart of the matter. It is not enough to discuss whether the empty tomb should be accepted historically. Augustine for one would have wanted to know what the empty tomb might convey theologically and symbolically. At the start of this chapter (and earlier in Chapter 2), we saw him comparing 'the daily miracle' of babies being born with the resurrected being brought alive 'from the tomb'. I can think of at least three ways in which we could satisfy a desire to grasp what the empty tomb of Jesus signified and symbolized.

First, where tombs express the finality and irrevocable loss of death, the open and empty tomb of Jesus symbolized the fullness of the new and everlasting life into which he had risen. Here the emptiness of the tomb paradoxically indicated the fullness of life into which the risen Jesus had entered. Graves naturally suggest the quiet decay of an existence dissolved by death. The empty tomb symbolized the opposite, the complete and new life that had overcome the silence of death.

Second, the emptiness of Jesus' grave reflects the holiness of what it once held, the corpse of the incarnate Son of God, who lived totally for others and died to bring a new covenant of love for all people. This 'Holy One' could not experience 'corruption' (Acts 2: 27 citing Ps. 16: 8–11). Addressing God with laconic brevity, Augustine drew attention to the identity and redemptive work of the Holy One, which justified the emptiness of his tomb: 'you will not allow the sanctified body, through which others are to be sanctified, to undergo decay' (en. Ps. 15.10).[29]

---

[29] *Expositions of the Psalms* (1–32), trans. Maria Boulding (Hyde Park, NY: New City Press, 2000), 184.

Third, the empty tomb expresses something vital about the nature of redemption: namely, that redemption is much more than an escape from our world of suffering and death. Still less is it a kind of second creation 'from nothing' (*ex nihilo*). Rather it means the transformation of this material, bodily world with its whole history of suffering and sin (see Rom. 8: 18–23). The first Easter began the work of bringing our universe home to its ultimate destiny. God did not discard the corpse of Jesus but mysteriously raised and transfigured it, so as to reveal what lies ahead for human beings and their world. In short, the empty tomb in Jerusalem forms God's radical sign that redemption is not an escape to a better world but a wonderful transformation of this world. Seen that way, the open and empty tomb of Jesus is highly significant for anyone who wants to appreciate what redemption through Christ means.

In a work occasioned by the death of his brother, St Ambrose of Milan (who baptized Augustine at Easter 387) expressed the cosmic impact of Christ's resurrection: 'in him [Christ] the world has risen, in him heaven has risen, in him the earth has risen' (*De excessu fratris sui Satyris*, 2.102; PL 16, 1403). Obviously so far one must say 'in Christ the world has partly but not wholly risen; in him the earth has risen but not already fully'. The empty tomb of Christ in Jerusalem may not yet have brought the actual resurrection of the whole world. Nevertheless it is nothing less than the enduring sign and symbol of how his resurrection has initiated the resurrection of the whole world.

The Making and Keeping of Easter Faith

When retrieving and updating Augustine's apology for faith in the risen Christ, we showed how Augustine set the gold standard for acknowledging the essential importance of 'background theories'. Without accepting that God is all-powerful and all-loving, the possibility of Easter faith is ruled out in advance. Furthermore, those who may agree in theory that God created the world but lack all wonder at the marvels of divine creation fatally narrow their chances of giving credence to the glorious identity-in-transformation that God effects in Jesus' resurrection from the dead.

Such an image of God differs sharply from the view of an 'outsider' God who does not or cannot suspend, let alone change, the operation of a closed system of causes and effects once they have come into being. In his *Confessions*, Augustine wrote of God or rather said to God: 'But you were more inward than my inward self (*tu autem eras interior intimo meo*)' (3.6.11). We might join with those who have paraphrased this remark as 'You were closer to me than I am to myself'. Being so 'within' human beings and all creation, God can be readily imagined as communicating gloriously new life to his crucified Son. Augustine's image of God, the vital background to his belief in the resurrection, is worlds away from that of a creator who has brought everything into existence but then acts like an 'absentee landlord' and allows natural causes to take care of the running of the universe.

Earlier sections of this chapter have argued the case for the historical reality of (1) the appearances of the risen Jesus and (2) the discovery of his empty tomb. The unexpected appearances to some individuals and groups formed the primary reason for the first followers of Jesus to accept his resurrection; the empty tomb constituted a confirmatory, secondary sign of his resurrection.

Admittedly in the case of both (1) and (2) the witnesses were a relatively small number of people. But it would make little or no difference if there were thousands of such witnesses. Stubborn sceptics, like David Hume (1711–76), would still argue that it is never rational to believe such witnesses and accept that a resurrection from the dead has happened. His (philosophical) background theory excludes in principle that God performs remarkable deeds, or at least that we could ever be rightly sure that such deeds have happened, even if there were a God capable of performing them. According to Hume, there could never be enough historical evidence to justify believing in Christ's resurrection from the dead.[30]

Hume's position has its value by reminding us that Easter faith is never decided simply on the basis of historical evidence alone. Even if

---

[30] See D. Hume, *An Enquiry concerning the Human Understanding*, ed. L. A. Selby-Biggs, X ('Of Miracles') (Oxford: Clarendon Press, 1963), 109–31, at 128. On problems with Hume's view of testimony, see C. A. J. Coady, *Testimony: A Philosophical Study* (Oxford: Clarendon Press, 1994), 79–100; on Hume's unsatisfactory reaction to 'astonishing reports', see ibid. 179–98.

millions of witnesses had claimed to have seen the risen Jesus and left abundant written testimony to report and support that claim, and even if Mary Magdalene and other women had left many authenticated letters about their discovery of the empty tomb, there would be more to believing in the risen Christ than such evidence from history.

But there are strong historical arguments for the resurrection, ones that include considerations that press beyond the New Testament witness to the Easter appearances and the discovery of the empty tomb. Often such an apologetic approach argues from demonstrable *effects* in history to the event of the resurrection as their only adequate or plausible *cause*. Chapter 2 recalled Augustine's particular version of this 'effect-to-cause' argument, one that finds counterparts in modern proposals coming from Christopher Evans, Hans Küng, Wolfhart Pannenberg, Richard Swinburne, and N. T. Wright.

Yet, apropos of these and other historical arguments, there is a story about Bertrand Russell, a nonbelieving philosopher, which enjoys its relevance. On being asked what his reaction would be if after death he found himself in the presence of God, Russell replied: 'I would say that God should have given me more evidence.' Russell would undoubtedly have said something similar if the question had been phrased in terms of finding himself after death in the presence of the risen Christ. Presumably Russell would have said, 'You should have given me more evidence in support of your resurrection.'

Here Maurice West wrote something that comments helpfully on a Russell-style position. In a novel, *The Clowns of God*, he described a conversation between a French pope and his sceptical German friend, Carl Mendelius. After debating some issues of faith, the pope remarks: 'Carl, old friend, there is never enough evidence.' Applying that remark to the present theme, we can say that there is never enough evidence for the resurrection, or—to put matters positively—that there is more to faith in the risen Jesus than knowing the (historical) evidence for his resurrection. Such faith, as Augustine knew very well, does not remain within the limits of evidence alone. Merely knowing the evidence and even finding it very persuasive does not yet mean knowing Jesus personally in faith.

Believing in the crucified and risen Jesus goes beyond accepting on evidence that something (namely, his resurrection) happened nearly two thousand years ago. Believing in him means entering here and now into a trusting, loving commitment to him. Ludwig Wittgenstein was on target when he wrote: 'it is love that believes the resurrection'.[31]

In working out the why and how of Easter faith, Augustine was at his best in bringing together love and light. He identifies 'the love of God poured into our hearts through the Holy Spirit' (Rom. 5: 5) with light: the love infused by the Spirit is also 'the light of the heart' (ep. 140.54).[32] This light enables 'an inner gazing of the heart' (s. 264.2), by which contemporary believers can see the risen Lord.[33]

Echoing and qualifying John's distinction between those (like the original Easter witnesses) who 'have seen and believed' and those who 'have not seen and yet have believed' (Jn. 20: 29), Augustine notes that 'we didn't see him hanging on the cross, nor observe him rising from the tomb', and adds at once: 'we hold this by faith; we behold it with the eyes of the heart' (s. 263.2).[34] Far from being the mere conclusion of a historical argument, Easter faith is then 'an inner gazing of the heart' or a seeing 'with the eyes of the heart', which the Holy Spirit, the love of God in person, makes possible. In that sense those who 'have not seen and yet have believed' have truly, mysteriously, and lovingly seen the crucified and risen Christ to whom they commit themselves.

---

[31] L. Wittgenstein, *Culture and Value*, trans. P. Winch (Oxford: Basil Blackwell, 1980), 33c.

[32] *Letters 100–155*, trans. Roland J. Teske (Hyde Park, NY: New City Press, 2003), 271.

[33] *Sermons* (230–272B), 227.

[34] Ibid. 220. No one, of course, 'observed' Christ 'rising from the tomb'. Augustine's words should be modified to read: 'nor observe him when he appeared to us gloriously risen from the tomb'.

5
Final Perspectives

The three volumes of *The Oxford Guide to the Historical Reception of Augustine*, edited by Karla Pollmann (2013), form a monumental achievement that illustrate the enduring significance of Augustine's teaching in many sections of Christian theology and human thought. What he preached and wrote have left a lasting mark on the interpretation of such themes as free will, grace, original sin, the sacraments, the Trinity, and truth. Sadly and a bit strangely, his Christology in general and presentation, in particular, of Christ's rising from the dead have suffered from much neglect. A desire to remedy this situation has motivated the writing of this book.

Unlike his influential mentor Ambrose of Milan, Augustine did not write even a short treatise on the resurrection. We glean his teaching on the resurrection of Jesus Christ by examining many of his works, which also come in different literary forms: *Answer to Faustus a Manichean*, *The City of God*, *Expositions of the Psalms*, *Homilies on the Gospel of John*, *Letters*, *Sermons*, and *The Trinity*. This research has, however, an important advantage. It alerts readers to the central importance of Christ's resurrection that pervades Augustine's thinking over many years and through a broad range of his works. The example of Augustine continues to raise the question: are contemporary theologies that fail to honour the centrality of Christ's glorious resurrection from the dead true to the Easter witness of the first Christians?

Beyond question, the concerns and gains of modern biblical scholarship can and should add to and correct what Augustine taught on such matters as the appearances of the risen Christ and the discovery of his empty tomb. 'Seeing' dominates what the New Testament reports about the disciples' post-resurrection encounters with Jesus. By concentrating on the possibility of 'touching' the risen body, Augustine had little to say about the risen Christ 'appearing' or 'letting himself be seen' by individuals (such as Mary Magdalene and Simon Peter) or groups of disciples (above all, 'the twelve'). More needs to be said about the nature and historicity of these Easter appearances.

The secondary sign of Christ's resurrection from the dead, the discovery of the empty tomb, has been widely debated in modern times. Augustine does not contribute much to these debates. His brief comments on the Holy One not undergoing 'corruption', however, can feed into a theology of the empty tomb—an essential task that should complement any discussion about the historicity of the open and empty tomb.

Even more than Origen, Augustine argued for the truth of Christ's resurrection from the dead by underlining public, historical facts that call for explanation. Despite its being proclaimed by uneducated people from the margins of society, the message of the resurrection came to be widely accepted. The human resources of the first disciples could not explain the successful propagation of the Easter message. Augustine argued from observable effects to their only plausible cause, the truth of the resurrection itself. This 'effect-cause' apologetic can be filled out further (for example, by noting the scandalous nature of proclaiming a *crucified criminal* as vindicated by God through resurrection), but it has not lost its plausibility. In recent times notable writers (such as Wolfhart Pannenberg, Richard Swinburne, and N. T. Wright) have developed different forms of such an 'effect-cause' case for Jesus' resurrection from the dead.

But Augustine knew that merely historical arguments do not produce faith in the crucified and risen Jesus. We need to 'see him with the eyes of our hearts'. Anticipating by many centuries Ludwig Wittgenstein ('it is love that believes the resurrection'), Augustine championed the essential role of love towards knowing and believing in Jesus gloriously resurrected from the dead.

Arguably the most significant contributions Augustine made to Christian thinking about the resurrection of Jesus concern (a) what preceded and (b) what followed that resurrection. (a) Over and over again Augustine highlighted God's creative activity. Unless one accepts God as the all-powerful and all-loving Creator, faith in the resurrection remains excluded. Augustine also encouraged his audience to renew their sense of awed wonder at the marvels of the created world. Nowadays the discoveries of modern science (as in the areas of astronomy, biology, and physics) make possible a richer and deeper sense of astonishment. Augustine knew that such wonder opens people up to the extraordinary 'wonder' of the resurrection.

(b) Unlike many theological successors, Augustine held together resurrection *and ascension*. The risen and exalted Christ lives forever as the primary minister of the Church's sacraments, the High Priest who intercedes for us, and the Head of the glorious *Totus Christus*. In recent times, a widespread lack of attention to the ascension has gone hand in hand with a neglect of Christ's role as eternal mediator and priest. It is in this area that Augustine's fully deployed theology of the resurrection maintains its lasting challenge and significance.

Let me finish on a personal note by noting with regret something that Augustine never wrote on the resurrection of Jesus. My favourite passage in all his writings comes when he addresses God in *Confessions* 10.6:

> What is it that I love when I love you? Not the beauty of a body nor the glory of time; not the brilliance of light so pleasing to the eyes; nor the sweet melodies of all kinds of songs; nor the fragrance of flowers, ointments, and perfumes; not manna and honey; nor limbs that welcome the embrace of the flesh. I do not love these when I love my God. And yet I love a kind of light, a kind of voice, a kind of fragrance, a kind of food, and a kind of embrace when I love my God, who is light, voice, fragrance, food, and the embrace of my inner person. There shines into my soul what no place can hold; there shines forth that which time cannot take away; and there is a fragrance that no breeze can disperse, a taste that eating does not diminish, and a clinging together that never loses its satisfaction. It is this that I love when I love my God.
>
> (translation mine)

Augustine never put a similar question: What do I love when I love Christ risen from the dead? Augustine knew that the light, the voice, the fragrance, the taste, and the touch of the glorious Jesus can fill our hearts in a complete and lasting way. It is a pity that he never expressed what our spiritual senses experience when they see, hear, smell, taste, and touch the risen Christ.

Select Bibliography

(a) Works on Augustine

Mamerto Alfeche, 'The Basis of Hope in the Resurrection of the Body according to Augustine', *Augustiniana* 36 (1986), 240–96.

Mamerto Alfeche, 'The Use of Some Verses in 1 Cor. 15 in Augustine's Theology of Resurrection', *Augustiniana* 37 (1987), 122–86.

Mamerto Alfeche, 'The Rising of the Dead in the Work of Augustine (1 Cor. 15: 35-7)', *Augustiniana* 39 (1989), 54–98.

Mamerto Alfeche, 'Augustine's Discussions with Philosophers on the Resurrection of the Body', *Augustiniana* 45 (1995), 95–140.

Marie-François Berrouard, *L'Integrité de la nature humaine du Christ après sa resurrection* (Paris: Institut d'Études Augustiniennes, 1977).

Andrea Bizzozero, *Il mistero pasquale di Gesù e l'esistenza credente nei Sermones di Agostino* (Frankfurt: Peter Lang, 2010).

Peter Brown, *Augustine of Hippo*, 2nd edn. (Berkeley, CA: University of California Press, 2000).

Nello Cipriani, 'Rhetoric', in Allan D. Fitzgerald (ed.), *Augustine through the Ages: An Encyclopedia* (Grand Rapids, MI: Eerdmans, 1999), 724–6.

Brian E. Daley, 'Christology', in Allan D. Fitzgerald (ed.), *Augustine through the Ages: An Encyclopedia* (Grand Rapids, MI: Eerdmans, 1999), 164–9.

Miles Hollingworth, *Saint Augustine of Hippo: An Intellectual Biography* (Oxford: Oxford University Press, 2013).

Helmut Hoping, 'Christology', in Karla Pollmann (ed.), *The Oxford Guide to the Historical Reception of Augustine*, ii (Oxford: Oxford University Press, 2013), 781–6.

George Lawless, 'Augustine and Human Embodiment', in Bernard Bruning et al. (eds.), *Collectanea Augustiniana: Mélanges T. J. van Bavel* (Leuven: Leuven University Press, 1990), 167–86.

Joanne McWilliam (ed.), *Augustine: From Rhetor to Theologian* (Waterloo, ON: Wilfrid Laurier University Press, 1992).

William H. Marrevee, *The Ascension of Christ in the Works of St Augustine* (Ottawa: University of Ottawa Press, 1967).

Suzanne Poque (ed. and trans.), *Augustin d'Hippone, Sermons pour la Pâque*, Sources Chrétiennes 116 (Paris: Cerf, 1966).

Hanne Roer, 'Rhetoric', in Karla Pollmann (ed.), *The Oxford Guide to the Historical Reception of Augustine* iii (Oxford: Oxford University Press, 2013), 1650–7.

Cristina Simonetti, *La risurrezione nel De Trinitate di Agostino: presenza, formulazione, funzione*, Studia Ephemeridis Augustinianum 73 (Rome: Augustinianum 2001).

Rowan Williams, *On Augustine* (London: Bloomsbury, 2016).

For extensive bibliographies of works by Augustine and works on Augustine, see Joseph T. Kelley, *What Are They Saying About Augustine?* (Mahwah, NJ: Paulist Press, 2014).

(b) The Resurrection of Jesus

Dale C. Allison, *Resurrecting Jesus: The Earliest Christian Tradition and Its Interpreters* (New York: T. & T. Clark, 2005).
Stephen Barton and Graham Stanton (eds.), *Resurrection* (London: SPCK, 1994).
Joseph W. Bergeron and Gary R. Habermas, 'The Resurrection of Jesus: A Clinical Review of Psychiatric Hypotheses for the Biblical Story of Easter', *Irish Theological Quarterly* 80 (2015), 157–72.
Reimund Bieringer et al. (eds.), *Resurrection in the New Testament: Festschrift for Jan Lambrecht* (Leuven: Leuven University Press, 2002).
James H. Charlesworth et al. (eds.), *Resurrection: The Origin and Future of a Biblical Doctrine* (New York: Continuum, 2006).
Stephen T. Davis, Daniel Kendall, and Gerald O'Collins (eds.), *Resurrection: An Interdisciplinary Symposium on the Resurrection of Jesus* (Oxford: Oxford University Press, 1997).
Robert Dale Dawson, *The Resurrection in Karl Barth* (Aldershot, UK: Ashgate, 2007).
Georg Gasser (ed.), *Personal Identity and Resurrection: How Do We Survive Our Death?* (Burlington, VT: Ashgate, 2010).
Gary R. Habermas, *The Risen Jesus and Future Hope* (Lanham, MD: Rowman & Littlefield, 2003).
Anthony J. Kelly, *The Resurrection Effect: Transforming Christian Life and Thought* (Maryknoll, NY: Orbis, 2008).
Michael R. Licona, *The Resurrection of Jesus: A New Historiographical Approach* (Downers Grove, IL: IVP Academic, 2010).
Ted Peters, Robert J. Russell, and Michael Welker (eds.), *Resurrection: Theological and Scientific Assessments* (Grand Rapids, MI: Eerdmans 2002).
Bernard Prusak, 'Bodily Resurrection in Catholic Perspectives', *Theological Studies* 61 (2000), 64–105.
Joseph J. Smith, 'N. T. Wright's Understanding of the Nature of Jesus' Risen Body', *Heythrop Journal* 57 (2016), 29–73.
Richard Swinburne, *The Resurrection of God Incarnate* (Oxford: Oxford University Press, 2002).
Jean-Pierre Torrell, *Résurrection de Jésus et résurrection des morts* (Paris: Cerf, 2013).
N. T. Wright, *The Resurrection of the Son of God* (London: SPCK, 2003).

Select Bibliography

(c) Gerald O'Collins on the Resurrection of Jesus Christ

Jesus Risen: An Historical, Fundamental, and Systematic Examination of Christ's Resurrection (Mahwah, NJ: Paulist Press, 1987).

Interpreting the Resurrection (Mahwah, NJ: Paulist Press, 1988).

'Newman's Seven Notes: The Case of the Resurrection', in Ian T. Ker and Alan G. Hill (eds.), *Newman After a Hundred Years* (Oxford: Clarendon Press, 1990), 337–52.

(With Daniel Kendall), 'The Uniqueness of the Easter Appearances', *Catholic Biblical Quarterly* 54 (1992), 287–307.

The Resurrection of Jesus: Some Contemporary Issues (Milwaukee: Marquette University Press, 1993).

'The Risen Jesus: Analogies and Presence', in Stanley E. Porter, Michael A. Hayes, and David Tombs (eds.), *Resurrection* (Sheffield: Sheffield Academic Press, 1999), 195–217.

'The Resurrection of Jesus: The Debate Continued', *Gregorianum* 81 (2000), 589–98.

Believing in the Resurrection: The Meaning and Promise of the Risen Christ (Mahwah, NJ: Paulist Press, 2012).

'Peter as Witness to Easter', *Theological Studies* 73 (2012), 263–85.

'The Appearances of the Risen Christ: A Lexical-Exegetical Examination of St Paul and Other Witnesses', *Irish Theological Quarterly* 79 (2014), 128–43. This article and 'Peter as Witness to Easter' were reprinted in *Christology: Origins, Developments, Debates* (Waco, TX: Baylor University Press, 2015).

A Biblical Index

The Old Testament

Genesis
5: 24 49
18: 1–8 14
18: 1–9 35
18: 22 14
19: 1 14

2 Kings
2 91
2: 9–12 49

Psalms
16: 8–11 110
19: 5 6
19: 10 25
44 18
65 21
101 2
120 2

Daniel
10: 10 77n.
10: 12 77n.
12 109

Tobit
12: 15 14
12: 17 77n.
12: 19 15

2 Maccabees
7 109

The New Testament

Matthew
11: 10 78
13: 47 42n.
18: 20 83
22: 29–30 19n.
22: 30 18
23: 39 92
27: 3–10 66
28: 4 100
28: 7 78
28: 8–10 11
28: 9 76
28: 9–10 100, 104
28: 10 78
28: 15 64
28: 16–20 67
28: 17 78

Mark
1: 2 78
1: 2–3 109
1: 16 102
1: 19 102
5: 24–34 11
8: 29 47
8: 31 5, 47
9: 31 5
10: 34 5
11: 1–10 47
15: 34 46
15: 40 108
16: 1–8 90, 92, 93, 107, 108, 109
16: 7 67, 78, 100, 108
16: 9 79
16: 9–11 100
16: 11 79
16: 12 79
16: 14 79

Luke
5: 27 102
7: 24 78
7: 27 78
9: 16–17 80
13: 35 92
19: 3–4 102
24 75, 79, 100
24: 13–35 67, 100, 104
24: 19 76
24: 23 104
24: 26 80
24: 31 9, 78
24: 33–49 100

Luke (*cont.*)
24: 34 67, 77, 100
24: 36–40 43
24: 36–43 103
24: 37 76n., 78
24: 39 10, 11, 43, 76, 78
24: 42–3 13, 79, 80
24: 43 13, 14
24: 50–1 43n.

John
1: 39 102
2: 19 5
4: 24 74
5: 21 5
5: 28–9 5
6: 39–40 5
9: 1–41 102
9: 37–8 102
10: 17–18 5
10: 18 5
11: 25 5
11: 38–44 7
11: 49 66
12: 21 102
12: 23–4 40
14: 17 57
16: 13 57
20 93
20: 1–2 50, 107, 108
20: 11–18 100
20: 11–19 67
20: 12 78
20: 14 78
20: 15 101
20: 17 11, 76
20: 18 78
20: 19 8, 9
20: 19–23 100
20: 20 11, 76n.
20: 22 24
20: 24–5 103
20: 24–9 67
20: 27 10, 11, 12, 43, 76
20: 28 102
20: 28–9 76
20: 29 78, 114
21 67, 79
21: 1 78
21: 1–14 80, 100, 104
21: 2 42n.
21: 9–14 79
21: 11 42n.
21: 13 13n.
21: 14 78

Acts
1: 3 79
1: 3–5 100
1: 4 13, 14, 79
1: 6–11 43n.
2: 27 110
4: 13 42n.
9 57n., 67
9: 1–9 100, 104
9: 7 100
9: 17 77
9: 27 78
10: 4 79
10: 40–1 13, 79
10: 40–2 100
10: 41 14
13: 31 77, 100
20: 7 49
22 57n., 67
22: 9 100
26 57n., 67
26: 14 100
26: 16 77

Romans
1: 3–4 73
4: 24 73
5: 5 58, 114
5: 6 73
6: 4 4, 24, 50
6: 10 5, 101
8: 9 73
8: 9–11 73
8: 10–11 5, 73
8: 18–23 111
8: 34 93
10: 9 2, 3, 5, 6, 29, 70
10: 17 57

1 Corinthians
1: 23 45, 47
2: 10–13 57
6: 14 4
9: 1 67, 78, 100, 101, 102, 104
11: 23–6 49
12: 3 74
15: 3–5 70
15: 5 67, 77, 100, 101, 104

A Biblical Index

15: 5–8 78
15: 6 67, 77, 100, 104
15: 7 77, 100, 104
15: 7–8 104
15: 8 67, 77, 100, 104
15: 20 99
15: 20–8 48
15: 23 99
15: 37–8 40
15: 44 9
15: 45 7n.
15: 50 9n.
15: 51–2 9
15: 53 9n.
16: 2 49

2 Corinthians
4: 6 57
4: 14 73
13: 4 5

Galatians
1: 1 4, 73, 101
1: 12 67, 101, 104
1: 13–14 104
1: 15–16 67, 101
1: 16 104
3: 13 45, 47
4: 4 73
4: 6 74
4: 14 78

Ephesians
1: 18 58n.
5: 8 57
5: 23 28

Philippians
2; 9 73, 91, 93
2: 11 73
3: 6 104

1 Thessalonians
1: 10 73

1 Timothy
3: 16 77, 91, 93

Hebrews
7: 25 93
9: 3 27
9: 7 27
13: 12–13 45, 47

1 Peter
1: 8 78
1: 21 4
2: 9 28

1 John
1: 1–3 16n.

Revelation
1: 16 77n.
1: 17–19 77
1: 20 77n.

An Index of Names

Alfeche, M. 3n., 4n., 119
Allison, D. C. 106n., 119
Ambrose of Milan, St 111, 115
Aquinas, St Thomas 23, 59n., 62, 72, 88
Arbesmann, R. 27n.
Arendt, H. 61
Aristotle 61, 62
Armstrong, D. M. 61
Ayala, F. J. 98n.
Ayres, L. 37n.

Babcock, W. 7n., 15n., 21n., 34n., 97n., 107n.
Bahrdt, C. F. 64
Baigent, M. 65
Barrett, C. K. 8n.
Barton, S. 120
Bauckham, R. 91
Behr, J. 53n.
Bergeron, J. W. 103n., 120
Berrouard, M.-F. 4n., 119
Bieringer, R. 120
Bizzozero, A. 4n., 119
Bonner, G. 25n.
Borchert, D. M. 84n.
Boulding, M. 2n., 18n., 19n., 20n., 26n., 55n., 70n., 94n., 110n.
Bowden, J. 103n.
Bradley, I. 39n.
Breuning, W. 82
Brown, P. 52n., 119
Brown. R. E. 42n.
Bruning, B. 119
Bultmann, R. 4
Bussanich, J. 55n.
Bynum, C. W. 88

Caravaggio 68
Celsus 44, 50, 53, 68, 99, 102–3
Chadwick, H. 44n., 50n., 68n., 99n., 102n.
Charlesworth, J. H. 120
Cicero, Marcus Tullius 55
Cipriani, N. 33n., 119

Clement of Rome, St 39, 52
Coady, C. A. J. 112n.
Collins, F. S. 97
Confucius 47
Consentius 7, 13n.
Craig, E. 84n.
Crouch, J. E. 64n., 72n.
Crum, J. M. C. 40

Daley, B. E. 119
Daly, E. J. 40n.
Danove, P. L. 92
Dante Alighieri 88n.
Danto, A. C. 84n.
Dardanus, Claudius Postumus 20
Davis, S. T. 49n., 87n., 120
Dawson, R. D. 120
Deogratias 7n.
Depril, W. 11n.
Derrett, D. 65
Divyanand, Soami 65
Dupont, A. 11n.
Dych, W. V. 55n.

Eardley, P. S. 55n.
Ebbeler, J. 5n.
Edwards, M. J. 62n.
Edwards, P. 84n.
Eliot, G. 56n.
Eliot, T. S. 60n.
Evans, C. F. 48, 113

Faustus a Manichean 1, 3, 7n., 9, 10n., 29, 35, 36, 115
Feuerbach, L. 56
Fitzgerald, A. D. 7n., 8n., 14n., 22n., 33n., 37n., 38n., 55n., 57n., 62n., 66n., 68n., 119
Fitzmyer, J. A. 51n., 102n.
Flint, T. P. 92n.
Flori, E. 14n.
Foucault, M. 60n.
Fraser, R. S. 99n.

An Index of Names

Garrett, B. 84n.
Gasser, G. 88n., 120
Gautama 46
Goodman, M. F. 84n.
Graves, R. 65
Gregersen, N. H. 80–1
Gregory the Great, St 58
Gregory of Nyssa, St 88n.
Grobel, K. 4n.

Habermas, G. R. 103n., 120
Harmless, W. 25n.
Harris, M. J. 57n.
Harrison, S. 66n.
Hastings, A. 39n.
Hayes, M. A. 121
Heidegger, M. 60n., 62
Hess, R. S. 49n.
Hick, J. 61
Hill, A. G. 121
Hill, E. 2n., 3n., 5n., 19n., 32n., 33n., 36n., 39n., 44n., 45n., 46n., 55n., 64n., 69n., 73n., 84n., 94n., 97n.
Hill, W. 73
Hitler, A. 60
Hoffmann, R. J. 99n.
Hollingworth, M. 119
Hoping, H. 119
Hopkins, G. M. 98
Hume, D. 112
Hunter, D. G. 8n., 12n.
Hutchison, W. G. 68n.

Ignatius of Antioch, St 10n.
Irenaeus, St 8n., 84, 86

James, C. 60n.
Januarius 21n.
Johnson, L. T. 78n.
Johnstone, B. 71
Jones, D. J. 25n., 87n.
Jones, M. K. 94n.
Joyce, D. 65
Jung, C. G. 60n.

Keener, C. S. 51n., 80n.
Kelley, J. T. 33n., 120
Kelly, A. J. 94, 120
Kendall, D. 5n., 49n., 65, 87n., 120, 121
Kennedy, R. 66n.

Ker, I. T. 121
Kirchberger, C. 59n.
Kleinschwärzer-Meister, B. 62, 96n.
Koester, C. R. 47n., 77n.
Küng, H. 46–7, 62, 66, 113

Lawless, G. 119
Lawrence, D. H. 65
Leftow, B. 87
Leigh, R. 65
Lennox, J. C. 97n.
Lewis, C. S. 60–1
Licona, M. R. 120
Lincoln, A. T. 76n.
Lincoln, H. 65
Locke, J. 84
Lonergan, B. F. 59
Lüdemann, G. 103–4, 106
Luz, U. 64n., 72n.

Marcus, J. 108
Marion, J.-L. 60n.
Marrevee, W. H. 4n., 119
Marshall, I. H. 78n.
Martinez, G. 71
McGahern, J. 83
McGrath, A. E. 97n.
McWilliam, J. 119
Mason, A. 39n.
Mayer, C. P. 25n.
Meyers, M. A. 98n.
Monica, St 83
Montgomery, W. 64n.
Moore, G. 65
Muhammad 46
Müller, H. 29n.

Newman, Blessed John Henry 121
Nichols, A. 86n.
Niebuhr, R. 60n.
Niederbacher, B. 88
Nolland, J. 64
Norris, R. A. 7n.
Novakovic, L. 4n.
Nussbaum, M. 61

Origen 44, 50, 52–3, 68, 102n., 116

Pannenberg, W. 48–9, 113, 116
Paulus, H. E. G. 65

An Index of Names

Penelhum, T. 84n.
Perkins, P. 64n.
Peter Lombard 23
Peters, T. 98n., 120
Pine-Coffin, R. S. 83n.
Plato 34, 37, 61, 62n.
Plotinus 34
Pollmann, K. 14n., 33n., 51n., 60n., 61, 62n., 66n., 96n., 115, 119
Poque, S. 119
Porphyry 34, 99
Porter, S. E. 121
Priebe, D. A. 49n.
Prusak, B. 120
Pullman, P. 65–9, 72, 107
Pyper, H. 39n.
Pythagoras 34

Quinn, E. 46n.
Quinn, J. D. 78n.

Radner, E. 51n.
Rahner, K. 55–6, 60n., 62, 96
Ratzinger, J. 60n., 86
Rees, D. 105–6
Reimarus, H. 99
Rembrandt 68
Renan, E. 68
Richard of St Victor 58–9
Roer, H. 33n., 119
Rotelle, J. E. 29n.
Russell, B. 113
Russell, R. J. 98n., 120

Schierl, P. 51n.
Schildgen, B. D. 63n.
Schleiermacher, F. E. D. 65
Scholl, S. 60–1
Schonfield, H. 65
Schweitzer, A. 64–5
Schwienhorst-Schönberger, L. 63n.
Selby-Biggs, L. A. 112n.
Simonetti, C. 3n., 119
Smith, D. A. 90–2, 107, 108n., 109
Smith, J. J. 120
Staniforth, M. 10n., 40n.
Stanton, G. 120
Stoeger, W. R. 98n.

Stump, E. 92n.
Swinburne, R. 49n., 62, 96, 113, 116, 120

Talbert, C. H. 99n.
Tertullian 36n., 40n., 52
TeSelle, E. 57n.
Teske, R. J. 3n., 5n., 7n., 36n., 41n., 58n., 114n.
Te Velde, R. 62n.
Thiering, B. 65
Tillich, P. 60n.
Tombs, D. 121
Tomlin, R. S. O. 33n.
Torrance, T. F. 94–5
Torrell, J.-P. 120
Towner, P. H. 78n.
Trigg, J. W. 69n.

Updike, J. 65

Van Fleteren, F. 7n., 14n., 62n.
Venturini, K. H. 64, 65, 72
Vermes, G. 70–1
Vessey, M. 8n., 12n., 29n., 33n., 37n., 38n.

Wacker, W. C. 78n.
Wagner, J. 82n.
Waldstein, M. 86n.
Walsh, J. T. 49n.
Wayte, S. 4n., 59n.
Welker, M. 98n., 120
West, M. 113
Wetzel, J. 22n., 62n.
Whitlark, J. A. 4n.
Wilkins, L. L. 49n.
William of Saint-Thierry 58
Williams, R. 37n., 55–6, 61, 120
Williams, T. S. M. 65
Wilson, A. N. 68–9
Winch, P. 114n.
Wisse, M. 63n.
Wittgenstein, L. 60, 62, 114, 116
Wittmer-Butsch, M. 51n.
Wright, N. T. 49, 62, 64n., 96, 105, 113, 116, 120

Yarbro Collins, A. 92, 107, 109

Zumkeller, A. 25n.

The manufacturer's authorised representative in the EU for product
safety is Oxford University Press España S.A. of El Parque Empresarial
San Fernando de Henares, Avenida de Castilla, 2 - 28830 Madrid
(www.oup.es/en or product.safety@oup.com). OUP España S.A. also acts
as importer into Spain of products made by the manufacturer.
Printed and bound by CPI Group (UK) Ltd, Croydon, CR0 4YY

20/03/2026

02075330-0001